MATCH DAY

8462.

First published 2006
This edition published in 2008

Murray & Sorrell FUEL©
Design & Publishing
33 Fournier Street
London E1 6QE

www.fuel-design.com

Design: Murray & Sorrell FUEL

Scans: Happy Retouching
Printed in Hong Kong

Distributed by Thames & Hudson
ISBN 978-0-9558620-1-4

WITHDRAWN

THE FASHION
RETAIL ACADEMY
LIBRARY

Renewals:
020 7307 2367
library@fashionretailacademy.ac.uk

WITHDRAWN

15 GRESSE STREET LONDON

demy

FASHION RETAIL ACADEMY REGISTERED IN ENGLAND COMPANY NO. 5507547
REGISTERED OFFICE: 15 GRESSE STREET LONDON W1T 1QL

y.ac.uk

FUEL

CONTENTS

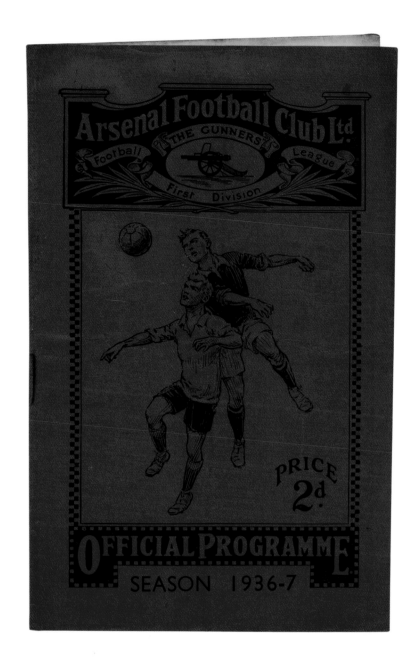

Arsenal Football Club Ltd.

THE GUNNERS

Football — League

First Division

PRICE 2d.

OFFICIAL PROGRAMME

SEASON 1936-7

PROGRAMMES AND GUNNERY
BRIAN GLANVILLE

For those of us who remain football romantics in this pragmatic age, match programmes are not remotely what they were. The soul has gone out of them. They mirror the age in their shiny, bulky, expensive form. Idiosyncrasy has alas gone out of the window. But perhaps we should console ourselves that this is one of the very few countries in the world where they still exist. Elsewhere, with the occasional exceptions of major international games, the match programme is largely unknown. I remember when in the early 1950s I lived in Florence and followed Fiorentina, there was a cursory sheet stuck in the seats, but it in no way reflected what we had in England.

I first became acquainted with football programmes during the war, and as you might have expected, they were essentially an ersatz phenomenon. Just one page for a penny. At White Hart Lane, where those eternal rivals Spurs and Arsenal were sharing a ground, Highbury having been taken over by the ARP and a barrage balloon unit – one poor airman was killed when a bomb landed on the training area where the balloons were flown – the exiguous programme was coloured somewhere between red and pink.

It meticulously gave the rank in the Army or Air Force of all the members of at least the home side. Arsenal had a number of commissioned officers in the Royal Air Force. Bernard Joy, always an amateur at centre half, was a Flight Lieutenant. Eddie Hapgood, left back and captain of England, Ted Drake, the barnstorming centre forward, and Jack Crayston, the elegant right half, were RAF officers too. Neither of the splendid Compton brothers was commissioned. Big Leslie, the older, an England full back in the latter stages of the war, was an army corporal. The supremely versatile Denis, a fine outside left and a still finer Test batsman, was some sort of sergeant major, I believe.

But programmes were by and large not much more than a rough guide to whom you were going to see; and that was, to some extent, the thrill of it. Service duties all too often caused players to drop out, but sometimes they would be excitingly replaced by stars on loan. During the war, guest players were an accepted phenomenon.

In those less sophisticated days, such changes were not announced over the tannoy. A little old man was entrusted with the wearing task of putting up the names and relevant numbers against the lower wall of the stands, with a series of yellow letters, each on its square black plate. I well remember the struggle the poor fellow had one Saturday, when the Gunner's guest at outside right was Liverpool's South African winger, Berry Nieuwenhuys!

There was still, however, room for programme notes on the back of the teamsheet, and in Arsenal's case they were written by their rotund and orotund manager, George Allison. Scant comparison here with the programme articles he contributed back in the 1920s, under the pseudonym of 'Gunner's Mate'. I remember just one item in the wartime notes. He referred to Len Shackleton, later to become celebrated as the Clown Prince of Soccer, a marvellous maverick whom Allison in fact, to Shack's bitter disappointment, had shown the door in 1939. Now, as Allison recorded, Shack was flourishing with Bradford Park Avenue – a solidly established club then, destined to knock Arsenal out of the FA Cup at Highbury in 1948, but subsequently and sadly to disappear from view. 'I remember,' wrote Allison, 'when this then frail boy was playing in our Enfield nursery.' This was a little ambiguous. Was he, I wondered, as an Arsenal fan, still an Arsenal player? I wrote to him for an autograph and asked. Back came my postcard with his signature and the curt message, 'I have no connection with Arsenal. My own club is Bradford.' He never, as he recounted in his subsequent autobiography, forgave Allison for patronising him – showing the supposed yokel a brand new television set – when he was given his dismissal.

Back, briefly, to the 1920s. I actually have an Arsenal programme for their return match against Spurs in 1922. Return, because, in those unwise days, the First Division clubs played each other home and away on successive Saturdays, with all the potential for resentment and revenge which such a silly fashion contained. The previous week, Arsenal, then a struggling club which, to Tottenham's fury, had crossed the river from Plumstead only in 1913, had come to White Hart Lane and won.

The Gunners' burly full backs, Hutchins and Bradshaw, had incurred the ire of the Spurs fans and led to one reporter writing, 'The crowd at once began to howl at the Arsenal players as if they were assassins. Can you wonder that the men from Highbury got a little rattled and out of hand?'

This was duly recorded in the programme by Gunner's Mate, who turned ferociously on a former referee who had dared to impugn Arsenal's methods. 'Those who remember his efforts in that capacity,' snarled the programme, 'would hesitate a long time before accepting him in his authority.' Equally castigated was a journalist who similarly attacked Arsenal's methods: 'The best criticisms of a match can hardly be expected from a gentleman holding a goodly number of shares in the contesting clubs.'

I shall go back further in time to examine the delightful excesses of the Arsenal programmes in the year they moved to Highbury, 1913, but in the meantime, what of Tottenham's? For many seasons after the war, their programmes consisted of a blue and white, printed affair, no photographs, which would eventually be devotedly edited by the late Leslie Yeates, an immensely busy freelance with a deep affection for the Spurs, after whom, for a while, the press room would be named. Though not always helped by the hierarchy, Les had the heart of the matter, knew Tottenham's history itself by heart, and has a proper, contemporary successor in Andy Porter: though Andy's well researched and intriguing 'blasts from the past' are overwhelmed by all those pages of commercial ads and ghosted reflections by the managerial staff. Like almost every other club.

The Spurs programme, in those earlier, post-war years, was not by any means always an anodyne publication. Above all, during the coruscating reign of the late Arthur Rowe, the outstanding, innovative manager of his time, the architect of the push and run, one touch methods which propelled Tottenham from the championship of the Second Division in 1950 to that of the top division in 1951. Such daring, exciting tactics were too much for a couple of resentful, embittered old directors, little Mr Herryot and tall, sombre, slightly sinister, Dewhurst Hornsby, notable if for nothing else for his eccentrically broad brimmed hats. Despite the huge success which the push and run methods, exemplified by the likes of inside left Eddie Baily and Welsh left half Ronnie Burgess, had brought the Spurs, these two malignant men resented them. They embarked on a campaign of sabotage, writing in the programme that in such and such a game they had been delighted to see the ball being kicked hard and long. Anathema to Rowe, who once asked, satirically, 'What *is* a good length ball?' A term of the times; though as Arthur pointed out, a good length ball could be of any length at all, if it reaches it's target.

Alas, Herriot and Hornsby would have their shabby victory. Arthur, once pre-war captain and centre half of Spurs, was a sensitive man, and such underhand criticism drove him finally into a nervous breakdown. He later became the manager of Crystal Palace, but there is no doubt that his most distinguished successor, Bill Nicholson, right half in the push and run team, learned plenty from him.

Back in the middle 1950s, I had my own problems with the Tottenham programme; forced to use it for an apology, when in fact I was all too unquestionably in the right. In those days, the talented Spurs reserve goalkeeper, who had joined them from Aldershot but found his way blocked in perpetuity by the majestic Ted Ditchburn – who recently died – was Ronnie Reynolds. I came to know Ronnie well, and one day he told me that, finding himself alone in the Tottenham office, he had a look at the books and found, to his astonishment, that they were paying their then manager – in fact a very poor one – Jimmy Anderson, a mere £20 a week and the club secretary, Reg Jarvis, a still more miserly £17.

This I wrote about in the weekly magazine *Sport Express*, for whom I was then the chief football correspondent. Tottenham were incensed. 'Diabolical, diabolical!' wheezed Dewhurst Hornsby to me, over the phone. Spurs demanded a retraction and an apology, or they would sue. I knew that every word we had published was true, but I was in a cleft stick. To justify what we had written, I would have to involve

Ronnie Reynolds, and that would be the end of his career at Tottenham. So I was obliged to bite the bullet, and to publish an apology and a withdrawal in the match programme. With retrospect, perhaps the best thing that could have happened to Ronnie Reynolds would have been to leave Tottenham where, for all his talents, he languished endlessly in the reserves.

Arsenal's programme at that time was vigorously and endearingly edited by Harry Homer, alias 'Marksman'. The successor to 'Recorder', alias W. M. Johnson, like Homer an Oxford graduate, who had edited the programme in the immediate pre-war years, with diligence, but without Harry's exuberant panache. Harry, like so many of the players, was an RAF officer in the war, serving some of it in Burma. When Highbury was closed down at the start of the war, those that remained there formed a team called Arsenal ARPS. Tom Whittaker, the much admired trainer who would in time become Arsenal manager, was among the players. Harry Homer figured on the wing with speed rather than guile. In fact I remember Cliff Bastin, an Arsenal hero whose 150 goals have only just been overtaken by Thierry Henry, telling me once that he envisaged Harry disappearing up Highbury Hill!

Harry's programme articles were replete with literary references. I recall him once quoting Oliver Goldsmith: 'I love everything that's old, old books...' Hard to imagine that being repeated now. He took strong moral attitudes, some of which may seem somewhat irrelevant in these cruder, coarser days. I remember him condemning an outburst of booing; yes folks, just booing; not obscene chanting, replete with four letter words. We must be rid, wrote Harry, of 'this apelike habit'.

From Charterhouse, my boarding school, I used to write him letters which always received a genial reply. Until, one golden day – doomed alas to be tarnished – he invited my father and myself to be his guests on Boxing Day, 1947, for the League match against Liverpool. Which, of course, the Gunners lost. This though they were then running away with the League. Red headed Albert Stubbins, the big Liverpool centre forward, scored both goals in a 2 – 1 defeat. Donkeys' years later, in his dotage, he sent me a message from his native Newcastle: 'Sorry to have spoiled your Boxing Day'. But at least Harry took me down to the dressing room where I saw the bruises on the shins of the centre forward Reg Lewis – 'Just a few little taps!' – and was even able to shake the hand, outside the dressing room – he hadn't played – of the heroic Denis Compton.

Travel back in time, and we find the Arsenal programmes – Allison still prominent – of their first game at Highbury. Doomed then, to the Second Division, having come horrifically bottom of the First with an abysmal record. Things, however, would improve.

Those programmes were redolent of a far more innocent age; though the horrors of the Great War and it's trenches were but a year away. In the first programme of all at Highbury, before the match against Leicester Fosse, even Gunners' Mate waxed lyrical, rather than acerbic.

'Gentlemen: our noble selves!' he enthused. 'I give you this toast by way of greeting on this auspicious day, which bids fair to mark the dawn of a new era and a great epoch in the career of Woolwich Arsenal. We are making our re-entry into the Second Division of the Football League with light hearts and unbounded optimism.'

Each programme contained a full page cartoon, featuring 'Dr. Highbury'. His diagnosis was ever positive. The weekly chat by the directors was similarly optimistic. 'Sirs,' was the opening quotation, 'you are very welcome to our house.' Photographed austerely in cutaway coat, you wonder what the schoolmaster captain and centre half of the team, Percy Sands, made of such florid quotation: 'It must appear in other way than words. Therefore I scant this breathing courtesy.' How different from the home life of our own dear North Bank.

For many years, Jack Helliar of East London printers, Hellier and Sons, not only printed the West Ham programme but edited and contributed to it; another who emphatically had the heart of the matter. When, on the eve of the Second World War, a bunch of West Ham players, like Bolton's, enlisted in the Territorials, Jack signed up too, passed A1; and never left these shores.

Just once, he was caught out. Looking back at past matches, he chose a league game, West Ham 3 – Newcastle United 5, describing it in dramatic terms. In fact it was a match notorious for the fact that suspicious bookmakers refused to pay out on it. It was common knowledge at the time that a certain unemployed coach and a certain member of the defence had been deeply embroiled. But by and large, Jack gave his programme colour and romance. It was a sad but all too significant day when he, a huge, ever amiable press steward, was brushed aside in favour of one of those anonymous publishers. But so, alas, it goes.

Chelsea's post-war programmes were predictably in blue and white with, on the front page a somewhat amateurish cartoon featuring a mascot, 'Billy Blue'. In January 1947 he was justifiably hymning the advent of the FA Cup, on the occaision of what turned out to be a thrilling game before a huge crowd of well over 60,000. A 1 – 1 draw. After the game I turned to a large man in the stand behind me and asked if I might buy his programme. 'Buy it?' he replied, in his generosity. 'You can have it!' I believe I still do. At that time, the front page, top right had corner, still had a cartoon of the head of a Chelsea Pensioner. Indeed the club for better or for worse was still nicknamed 'The Pensioners'. But when Drake, the former Arsenal centre forward, took over as manager in the summer of 1952, one of the first things he did was to take the Pensioner off the programme. In future, Chelsea would be 'The Blues'.

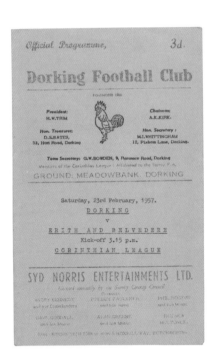

Official Programme, 3d.

Dorking Football Club

FOUNDED 1880

President:
H.W.TRIM

Chairman:
A.K.KIRK

Hon. Treasurer:
D.S.BATES,
33, Hart Road, Dorking

Hon. Secretary:
M.T.WHITTINGHAM
12, Pixham Lane, Dorking.

Team Secretary: G.W.BOWDEN, 9, Ranmore Road, Dorking
Members of the Corinthian League : Affiliated to the Surrey F.A.

GROUND: MEADOWBANK, DORKING

Saturday, 23rd February, 1957.

D O R K I N G
v
E R I T H   A N D   B E L V E D E R E
Kick-off 3.15 p.m.
C O R I N T H I A N   L E A G U E

SYD NORRIS ENTERTAINMENTS LTD.

REDHILL v FULHAM

— Tuesday 23rd, October 1976 K.O. 7.30 p.m.

Official Programme 20p.

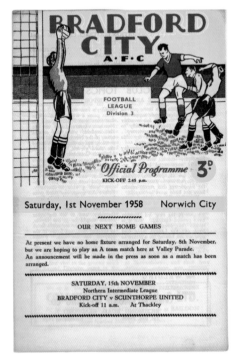

BRADFORD CITY A·F·C

FOOTBALL
LEAGUE
Division 3

Official Programme 3D
KICK-OFF 2.45 p.m.

Saturday, 1st November 1958   Norwich City

OUR NEXT HOME GAMES

At present we have no home fixture arranged for Saturday, 8th November,
but we are hoping to play an A team match here at Valley Parade.
An announcement will be made in the press as soon as a match has been
arranged.

SATURDAY, 15th NOVEMBER
Northern Intermediate League
BRADFORD CITY v SCUNTHORPE UNITED
Kick-off 11 a.m.   At Thackley

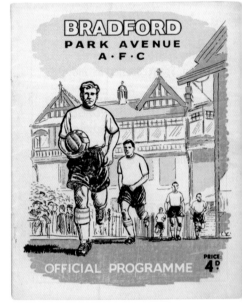

BRADFORD PARK AVENUE A·F·C

OFFICIAL PROGRAMME

PRICE 4D

INTRODUCTION
BOB STANLEY

The musky smell of a programme fair – so much damp plastic, the heating always a notch too high in an airless room – would make most people run for the hills. In the very male world of serious football programme collecting, aesthetics don't count for too much. Collectors will naturally concentrate on the club they support, often completing seasons they've attended and then working backwards until sanity and bank balances are called into question. I can't imagine how hard it would be to explain to your other half if you were, say, a Crewe Alexandra supporter, whose programmes were stubbornly dull for decades. Yet if you followed Middlesbrough, Crystal Palace, or either Bradford side, the programmes are undoubtedly beautiful objects. Of course, this will pass most people by – the few hundred Bradford Park Avenue fans may be aware of their club's artistically distinguished past, but that's not likely to earn them an exhibition at the Barbican.

Programmes are almost unknown to the general public, just something that might crop up in car boot sales in a box alongside old knitting patterns. *Match Day* aims to rescue the art of the football programme, concentrating on its peak years from the resumption of professional football in peacetime, 1945, to the beginning of the Premiership in 1992, when changing technology and the blind greed of the professional clubs changed them entirely. They morphed from home-made, A5 sociological pamphlets into something more suitable to an ice gala featuring obscure cast members from *EastEnders*.

I love football, but I've always found the ephemera at least as absorbing. Seventies FA Cup ties at Leatherhead and Sutton United would have been less significant without a rosette and, of course, a programme. When George Best came to Redhill for an unlikely midweek friendly, my dad couldn't take me to the match (not that I'm holding it against him... but I also missed the moon landing). Still, I made sure I picked up a spare programme the following Saturday – not to show off, but just because it seemed important to own a copy. That's the story of my life, a hoarder's bug that makes moving house ever more problematic.

It began with a box of programmes in the loft that used to be brought down on wet Saturdays, along with my mum's Bayko and my dad's knackered old accordion – such was the way to spend a weekend in post-austerity Surrey. There were plenty of Chelsea, Arsenal and Charlton, along with more esoteric programmes for speedway events, or Chris Barber's Jazz Band playing at Dorking Halls. Most treasured was a stack of Dorking FC programmes from the fifties, when it seemed they could annually win the Surrey Senior League at will. Dad had got the whole first team's autographs on one programme which – knowing now how scarce these things can be – might be unique. Certainly when he lent it to the club a few years back they were scarily reluctant to hand it back.

Ads for shops and long gone eateries like the Golden Milk Bar may as well have been from the Victorian age, but the statistics were what really grabbed me. League tables, leading scorers, stuff that still felt entirely relevant, and still does. Even looking at stats from a few years back can put clubs' futures and pasts into sharp relief.

A private pleasure became marginally more public when I found a like minded soul at school. Craig Jenkinson used to sit on his garden wall on the A23 and throw rotten apples at passing cars. He was a Brummie with few friends but a large collection of Midlands programmes, mainly Villa and Coventry. A Chelsea fan, like my dad, he borrowed our fifties stash (another championship season) and returned them with invented scores scribbled on the front of previously pristine ephemera – never less than five goals for the Blues, always a hat trick for Roy Bentley. My dad was pissed off, but – being selfish – this is where it really took off for me: the turn of the seventies was a high point in programme design. Not for Chelsea, maybe, but Peerless Press in the West Midlands were creating some beautiful things. The 'Cov' programmes, miraculously, Craig couldn't care less about and gave them to me. It would be a long while before I discovered about John Elvin and Sportsgraphic, but immediately the *Sky Blue* programmes seemed a significant discovery, a million miles away from Dorking's typed green paper, or even from those of the bigger clubs – the Arsenals and Chelseas – with their predictable action shots and ground photos.

Non-league football was what I was raised on, stuck in the heart of Surrey with only cocky Palace to the north representing the county at pro level, and nearby Guildford City in terminal decline by the time I was old enough to notice. Their amalgamation with Dorking – captured on a harrowing single sheet, one colour programme – sucked both clubs into the abyss and taught me the melancholy side of football early on. I was lured into the world of non-league during the 1974/75 season when then Southern League Wimbledon earned a goalless draw at Elland Road, Dickie Guy saving a Peter Lorimer penalty, at a time when Revie's Leeds were every bit as dully dominant as Mourinho's Chelsea. The same season saw shock cup results for Altrincham (drew with Everton), Wycombe Wanderers (drew with Middlesbrough) and Stafford Rangers who, like Wimbledon, made the fourth round.

Locally, Leatherhead – a small Surrey town with a squat, leafy, and frequently waterlogged ground at Fetcham Grove – beat Brighton away to also reach the fourth round where they faced Leicester City. They were drawn at home but switched the tie to Filbert Street. Watching the wrestling on *World of Sport*, the game was deemed important enough to warrant a scoreflash at the bottom of the screen once Leatherhead went 2 – 0 up. They were North Korea taking on Eusebio's Portugal in 1966: the Tanners versus Keith Weller and Frank Worthington. And like North Korea, they ran out of steam. Every time Mick McManus squealed as his ear was tweaked, a score flash came up. Agonisingly, it finished 3 – 2 to Leicester. When I asked for the programme at a fair in London a few years ago, the bloke behind the stall turned out to be David Reid, Leatherhead's centre half that day. The world rarely gets much smaller.

At the turn of the seventies, programme design reached a modernist high water mark. High contrast, dramatic images adorned covers, frequently two colour – nothing, as Berthold Lubetkin said, 'jazzy and hideous.' Club crests were banished in favour of serious looking men in simple, round collar shirts (kits, too, embraced a new minimalism). Kings of the era – any era, for me – were a Midlands company called Sportsgraphic. John Elvin had been working on West Brom's *Albion News* at the end of the sixties, and straight away made an impact with his German inspired landscape programme. Bernard Gallagher was a freelancer who produced Aston Villa's programme. Together they found an office above a garage in Birmingham.

Albion News won them awards, and soon Sportsgraphic were approached by Derek Robins at Coventry who, under Jimmy Hill's guidance, had gone from a perennial Third Division side to Europe. They had a new kit and nickname, and a flashy updated stadium which always stood out on *Match of the Day* because of the prominent bank of disabled cars in one corner – possibly, I suspect, because they were colour co-ordinated with the Sky Blues' kit. Bernard Gallagher remembers that Elvin was 'totally absorbed by his work. Completely wrapped up – very, very particular and accurate. He got programme design by the scruff of the neck.' Elvin trusted Gallagher, who took their designs to Peerless Press in West Bromwich, and hired an illustrator as well as cartoonist Frank 'Bristow' Dickens to write a strip called *Striker*. In Sportsgraphic's first year it won the Design and Art Directors' Award.

'Posters, montages, white out of black type – especially for floodlit matches. John was a clean worker. Everything spot on. Weird and wonderful typefaces he got set in London. He thought of everything.' Elvin designed the stats page, had a logo for the letter page, and used the programme (or 'magazine' as he called it) to vent his feelings. 'Being the editor of a club magazine can be likened in many ways to being the manager of a team. The club approaches 'the man' they want to do the job because they want him to do it the way they know only he can. Policies have to be laid down... the controversy still rages over *Sky Blue* magazine.' Elvin was not a man to compromise. At the end of his second year, Coventry gave Sportsgraphic the boot.

'He could sell any concept' remembers Gallagher, 'he was fairly relentless at pushing it and you'd almost give in at the end. I can imagine him rubbing people up the wrong way.' Knowing he'd already lost the job, Elvin crammed Coventry's last home programme of 1971 with bile directed against the club's stupidity. 'It was libellous. They were all destroyed. Coventry spent the morning tearing the pages out of the programme.' Bernard Gallagher retired from programme design in 2002, having worked at Aston Villa since 1971 as well as Norwich, Aberdeen, Rangers, Bristol City (from the First Division to the Fourth), Everton, and Leicester. John Elvin worked at Luton for a season, and designed Clive Everton's *Hockey Scene* and *Snooker Scene* for a while. 'He was in charge of the layouts, 1972 and '73' says Everton. Does he have any idea where the maverick might be today? 'I found him impossible to get on with. I haven't seen him for thirty years. I wish it was longer. Let's leave it at that.'

'I often think of John' says Bernard Gallagher. 'I obviously learnt a lot from him, but when a seventy year

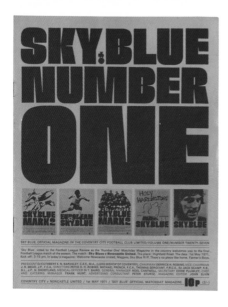

old pensioner would say 'I can't read this', I compromised but John wouldn't. He was married with three kids. One had a trial for Chelsea. The thing is, football is a visual game and John was a visualist.'

D.J. Taylor says that 'any social historian worth his salt who wanted to discover what English life was like in, say, the period 1966-79, that crucial World-Cup-to-Thatcher span, could do worse than assemble a couple of hundred football programmes.' Inside the covers, programmes could be less than exotic affairs. Liverpool issues from the height of the swinging sixties show a life not lived out inside E-Type Jags or the Scotch Of St James; hair is still nowhere near the collar. There might be the odd 'lovely lady' supporter who is doing well for herself with a residency in a Huyton boozehall, but no Beatles. Plenty of ads for local pubs, plumbers and pet shops, too, with a few words from the gaffer about the previous Saturday's goalless draw. And there is the half-time scoreboard, simple in theory, but in practice as hard to crack as the enigma code.

Of course, they also contain nuggets. Programme editors' columns usually err on the side of caution. They are an exercise in anger management. In a 1976 Darlington programme, Peter Boddy wrote a piece entitled 'Are The Press Destroying Football?' after Mike Langley of the *Sunday People* had 'advocated the extinction of the smaller club and the formation of a super league'. Boddy's anger is beautifully restrained: 'One remembers a similar view expressed in the

Sun newspaper a few years ago, when it suggested the league would be better off without the Quakers. Yet here we are, still ticking along, and now getting some success.' For Exeter City's game with Stockport County, the anonymous editor asks 'What went wrong? In my notes for the Southport programme I asked you to get behind City from the word go. Being a member of the Supporters' Association Committee, I sat by the Committee hut to judge the response to my appeal. I was disappointed! Perhaps you were overwhelmed because Eric Morecambe was at the match.' Yes Ed, that'll be it.

Adverts strain to incorporate football language. Luton Town, minutes from the Vauxhall car plant, claimed the Viva 'scores every time', a recurring pun. A little nattier – with interior and exterior shots of the vehicle – was 'outside right, inside right,' a strangely arcane pun in a world of diamond formations and players in the hole. More often, the ads verged on the surreal. Reading – aka the Biscuitmen – ran a Huntley and Palmers ad that read 'Kick-off with Cornish Wafers, at any time!' Adcocks (presumably a Fenland only beverage) stretched credulity by drawing a league table featuring only themselves and Peterborough United. 'Top the table with Adcocks Soft Drinks.' Adcocks are second in the table and have played no games. It is total gibberish. Murrays Bread and Cakes of Darlington clearly didn't run to any kind of budget and utilised child labour – at least, you'd hope the ad wasn't drawn by anyone over the age of eleven. Manchester City were the surprising recipients of Jamie Reid artwork when they hosted Derby County in December '76. In Derby, later that night, the Sex Pistols' Anarchy tour was meant to be rolling in – it was aimed at away fans who might find themselves at a loose

end when they got back to the East Midlands. Unfortunately for them, the gig was cancelled in the wake of their 'filth and the fury' live TV outburst.

Still it's the covers that excite. You don't need to know anything about Doncaster's away record in the 1970/71 season, or when West Brom ceased being known as the 'Throstles' and became the 'Baggies' to appreciate the artwork of a Sportsgraphic *Sky Blue* cover, or the folk art impact of Dover Athletic's designer. Frome Town's handiwork seems to be based on A.E. Marty's London Transport posters of the 1930s; a floodlit game is evoked almost religiously for an Arsenal vs Rotherham cup replay at Hillsborough; line drawings for Sheppey United and Slough Town viscerally capture the primeval urge to kick a ball, one of man's most basic desires.

This book doesn't attempt to pull out the rarest or most prized programmes for collectors; other publications have already catered for that market. Every league club from 1945–92 is included, but some of the most enigmatic examples are found outside the professional game. There are hundreds of non-league clubs – we have restricted ourselves to programmes of beauty and great moment.

Who would remember Coventry Sporting of the West Midlands Regional League unless they had beaten Tranmere Rovers in the first round of the 1975/76 FA Cup? Post-match, full back Charlie Sorbie let reporters into their secret: 'I hate poached eggs, but that's what we've had before the last two Cup rounds, so it had to be the same again.' The Tranmere side that day included future football names on the other side of the fence – the BBC's Ray Stubbs and disgraced FA executive Mark Palios – but Sporting folded, forgotten, in 1989. With no Accrington or Bradford Park Avenue style resurrection on the cards and their ground long gone, the programme is the most tangible proof of Coventry Sporting's existence.

Elsewhere, there is the psychedelic joy of Hampton's late sixties design, the eerily lifeless Rugby Town players, the ultimate DIY efforts of Deal Town. All have made more impact through individuality than some pro clubs have in generations. Odd quirks become apparent when you sift through a few dozen: how come the well supported Dover's programmes have always resembled a schoolchild's C minus graded project on dinosaurs, while near neighbours Folkestone clearly employed hirsute chaps from the local art college?

Sponsorship proved to be the downfall of the classic programme design. Advertising had never been a problem – a local brewery ad lent the likes of Crewe a touch of Disney fairy dust, so dull was their regular design. After a brief fling with the cumbersome newspaper format, Derby County's *Ram* switched from players at home with their families, to pictures of the first team grinning by a milk float; when Brian Clough was forced to cosy up to a Morris Marina with a come hither look, raw commercialism (surreal as it may now seem) ground its boot into the dreams of John Elvin. The Corinthian spirit rapidly ebbed away. First out of the blocks was the Watney Cup, played between seasons in 1971, the first sponsored football competition and proud of it. Little coincidence that the last FA Amateur Cup – which could pull a capacity crowd to Wembley just twenty years previously – ended in 1974, replaced by the semi-pro FA Trophy and the barely pro FA Vase for players on little more than travel expenses.

Liverpool's dalliance with Hitachi at the height of their European Cup winning powers showed just how little money there was in football in the eighties – a clock radio was the star prize for some lucky soul in a crowd of over 40,000. With crowds dwindling, many clubs abandoned stylish design, assuming there was no point in trying to lure fans in with a touch of class when they were scared of being caught in a hooligan scrum, or simply shunned at work. It's hard to imagine now just how ostracised football fans were in the eighties, before Italia '90 turned the sport's fortunes on its head. No question – the programmes reflect football's low self-esteem.

As with much lo-fi, DIY culture, the switch to digital graphics from the letterpress and genuine cut-and-paste was the very end. Even non-leaguers could now produce flashy programmes with high production values (I'm thinking of recent Barnet programmes which would grace a West End show) but lacking in charm. Like vinyl over downloads or caffs over Starbucks, choice and convenience have bred conformity and complacency. Bad colour schemes are everywhere because the extra colours don't cost anymore. A Hendon Supporters FC programme from 1979 has the production values of an Angry Brigade communique; that won't happen again in a hurry.

That the switch to digital largely coincided with the birth of the FA Premiership – the ultimate triumph of corporate greed over the Corinthian game of soccer – at

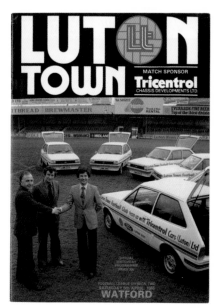

least gives us a handy bookend. Researching has involved delving into pre-war programmes which, to my shame, I'd always dismissed as little more than team sheets. I just hadn't seen that many, and I'm glad Brian Glanville has put the record straight. But these are the programmes of a defined era, football's greatest rise and fall. Either side of it are entirely different worlds. On top of which, try tracking down programmes for clubs with short-lived interwar league careers like Ashington and Thames. Just one programme for either club will set you back several hundred quid.

Me, I'm still happy picking up random beauties at ephemera fairs for a couple of quid, whether it's Bradford City or Bath City. I'm no completist. Unless, of course, you're about to offer me a complete run of *Sky Blues*, 1970/71.

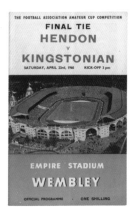

THE FOOTBALL ASSOCIATION AMATEUR CUP COMPETITION

FINAL TIE

HENDON

v

KINGSTONIAN

SATURDAY, APRIL 23rd, 1960   KICK-OFF 3 pm

EMPIRE STADIUM

WEMBLEY

OFFICIAL PROGRAMME   ·   ONE SHILLING

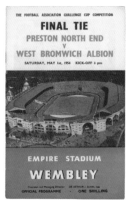

THE FOOTBALL ASSOCIATION CHALLENGE CUP COMPETITION

FINAL TIE

PRESTON NORTH END

v

WEST BROMWICH ALBION

SATURDAY, MAY 1st, 1954   KICK-OFF 3 pm

EMPIRE STADIUM

WEMBLEY

OFFICIAL PROGRAMME   ·   ONE SHILLING

THE FOOTBALL LEAGUE

CUP FINAL

QUEEN'S PARK RANGERS

VERSUS

WEST BROMWICH ALBION

(HOLDERS)

SATURDAY MARCH 4th, 1967

Kick-off 3.30 p.m.

EMPIRE STADIUM **WEMBLEY**

OFFICIAL PROGRAMME — ONE SHILLING

Incorporating Special Cup Final Issue of Football League Review

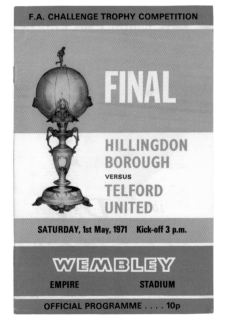

F.A. CHALLENGE TROPHY COMPETITION

FINAL

HILLINGDON BOROUGH

VERSUS

TELFORD UNITED

SATURDAY, 1st May, 1971   Kick-off 3 p.m.

WEMBLEY

EMPIRE   STADIUM

OFFICIAL PROGRAMME 10p

THE FOOTBALL LEAGUE

cup

ARSENAL v SWINDON TOWN

Saturday March 15 1969

Kick Off 3.30p.m.

final

OFFICIAL PROGRAMME TWO SHILLINGS

Incorporating Special Issue of Football League Review

WORLD CHAMPIONSHIP
JULES RIMET CUP

Final

ENGLAND v WEST GERMANY
SATURDAY · JULY 30 · 1966
EMPIRE STADIUM
SOUVENIR PROGRAMME WEMBLEY PRICE 2/6

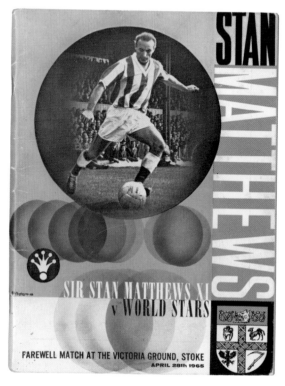

STAN MATTHEWS

SIR STAN MATTHEWS XI v WORLD STARS

FAREWELL MATCH AT THE VICTORIA GROUND, STOKE
APRIL 28th 1965

LEAGUE CLUBS

1945–1992

ACCRINGTON STANLEY

FOUNDED: 1878, reformed 1921, 1968
GROUND: Peel Park, Crown Ground
NICKNAME: Stanley

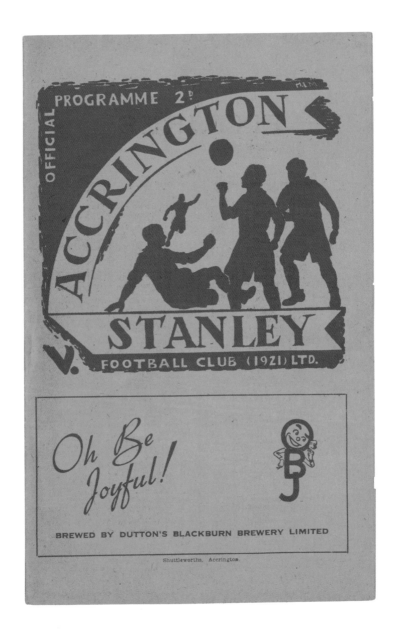

ALDERSHOT

FOUNDED: 1927
GROUND: Recreation Ground
NICKNAME: Shots

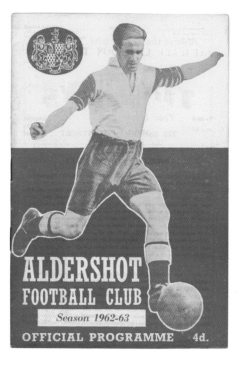

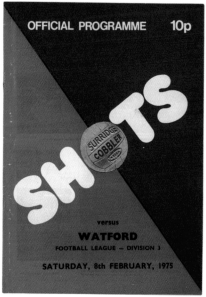

ARSENAL

FOUNDED: 1886
GROUND: Highbury
NICKNAME: The Gunners

LEAGUE CHAMPIONS: 1948, 1953, 1971, 1989, 1991
FA CUP WINNERS: 1950, 1971, 1979
LEAGUE CUP WINNERS: 1987
UEFA CUP WINNERS: 1970

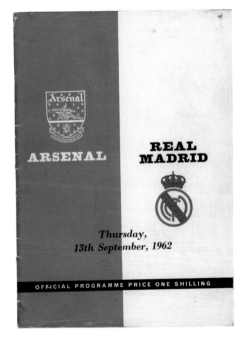

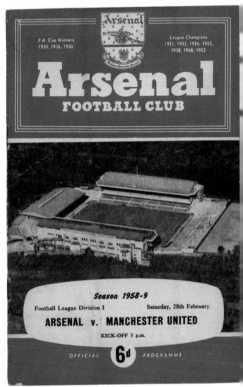

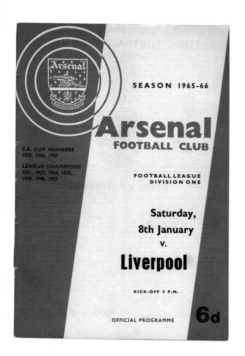

SEASON 1965-66

Arsenal
FOOTBALL CLUB

F.A. CUP WINNERS
1930, 1936, 1950

LEAGUE CHAMPIONS
1931, 1933, 1934, 1935,
1938, 1948, 1953

FOOTBALL LEAGUE
DIVISION ONE

Saturday,
8th January
v.
Liverpool

KICK-OFF 3 P.M.

OFFICIAL PROGRAMME **6d**

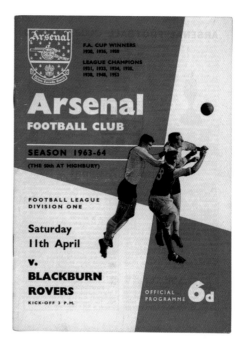

F.A. CUP WINNERS
1930, 1936, 1950

LEAGUE CHAMPIONS
1931, 1933, 1934, 1935,
1938, 1948, 1953

Arsenal
FOOTBALL CLUB

SEASON 1963-64
(THE 50th AT HIGHBURY)

FOOTBALL LEAGUE
DIVISION ONE

Saturday
11th April
v.
BLACKBURN
ROVERS

KICK-OFF 3 P.M.

OFFICIAL
PROGRAMME **6d**

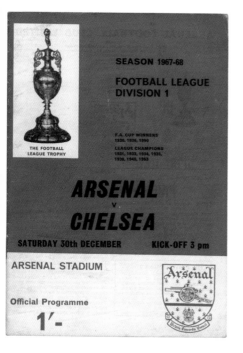

SEASON 1967-68

FOOTBALL LEAGUE
DIVISION 1

F.A. CUP WINNERS
1930, 1936, 1950

LEAGUE CHAMPIONS
1931, 1933, 1934, 1935,
1938, 1948, 1953

THE FOOTBALL
LEAGUE TROPHY

ARSENAL
v.
CHELSEA

SATURDAY 30th DECEMBER   KICK-OFF 3 pm

ARSENAL STADIUM

Official Programme

1'-

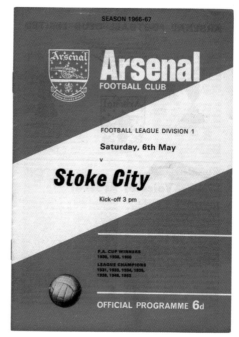

SEASON 1966-67

Arsenal
FOOTBALL CLUB

FOOTBALL LEAGUE DIVISION 1

Saturday, 6th May
v
Stoke City

Kick-off 3 pm

F.A. CUP WINNERS
1930, 1936, 1950

LEAGUE CHAMPIONS
1931, 1933, 1934, 1935,
1938, 1948, 1953

OFFICIAL PROGRAMME **6d**

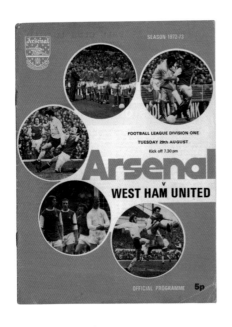

SEASON 1972-73

FOOTBALL LEAGUE DIVISION ONE

TUESDAY 29th AUGUST

Kick off 7.30 pm

Arsenal
v
WEST HAM UNITED

OFFICIAL PROGRAMME **5p**

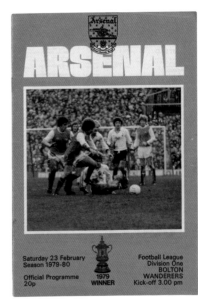

ARSENAL

Saturday 23 February
Season 1979-80

Official Programme
20p

1979
WINNER

Football League
Division One
**BOLTON
WANDERERS**
Kick-off 3.00 pm

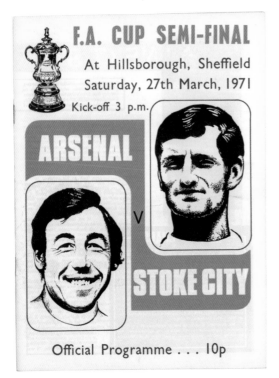

F.A. CUP SEMI-FINAL

At Hillsborough, Sheffield
Saturday, 27th March, 1971

Kick-off 3 p.m.

ARSENAL

v

STOKE CITY

Official Programme . . . 10p

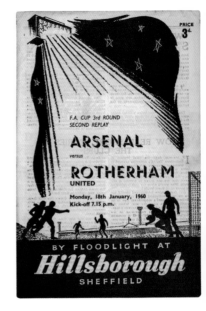

PRICE
3d.

F.A. CUP 3rd ROUND
SECOND REPLAY

ARSENAL
versus
ROTHERHAM
UNITED

Monday, 18th January, 1960
Kick-off 7.15 p.m.

BY FLOODLIGHT AT
Hillsborough
SHEFFIELD

ASTON VILLA

FOUNDED: 1874
GROUND: Villa Park
NICKNAME: The Villans

LEAGUE CHAMPIONS: 1981
FA CUP WINNERS: 1957
LEAGUE CUP WINNERS: 1961, 1975, 1977
EUROPEAN CUP WINNERS: 1982

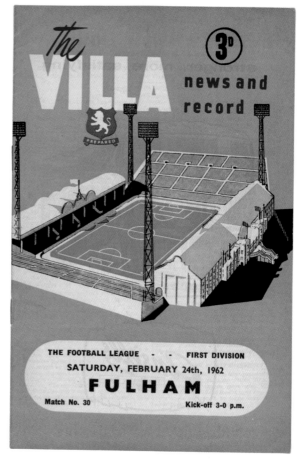

BARNET

FOUNDED: 1882
GROUND: Underhill
NICKNAME: The Bees

FA AMATEUR CUP WINNERS: 1946

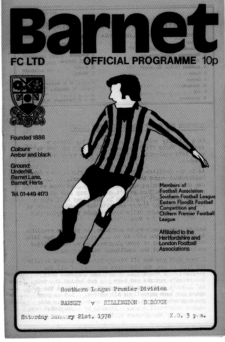

BARNSLEY

FOUNDED: 1887
GROUND: Oakwell
NICKNAME: The Tykes

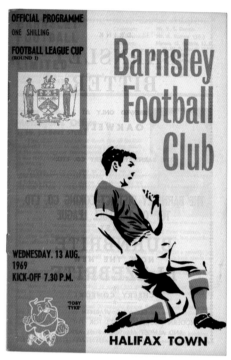

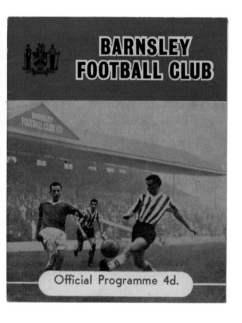

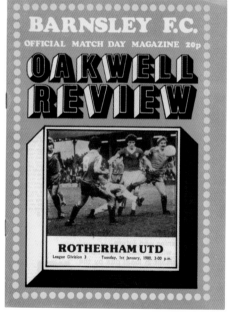

BARROW

FOUNDED: 1901
GROUND: Holker Street
NICKNAME: The Bluebirds

FA TROPHY WINNERS: 1990

Barrow AFC

HOLKER ST. GROUND
Barrow-in-Furness

OFFICIAL PROGRAMME 6d

SPATIARI UT PROGREDIARIS

Barrow AFC

HOLKER STREET GROUND
BARROW-IN-FURNESS

Official Programme 4d.

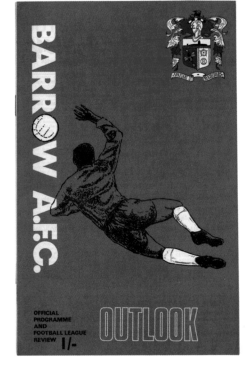

BARROW A.F.C.

OFFICIAL
PROGRAMME
AND
FOOTBALL LEAGUE
REVIEW 1/-

OUTLOOK

BIRMINGHAM CITY

FOUNDED: 1875
GROUND: St Andrews
NICKNAME: The Blues

LEAGUE CUP WINNERS: 1963

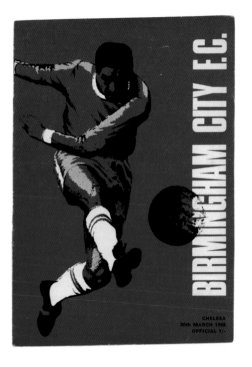

BLACKBURN ROVERS

FOUNDED: 1875
GROUND: Ewood Park
NICKNAME: Rovers

BLACKPOOL

FOUNDED: 1887
GROUND: Bloomfield Road
NICKNAME: The Seasiders, Tangerines

FA CUP WINNERS: 1953

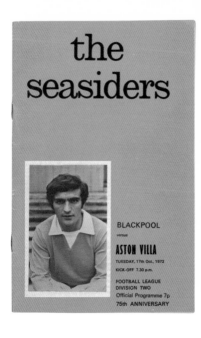

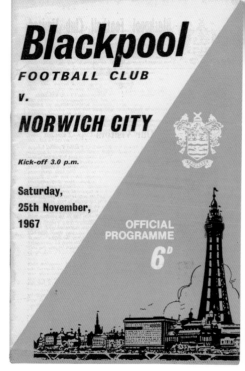

BOLTON WANDERERS

FOUNDED: 1874
GROUND: Burnden Park
NICKNAME: The Trotters

FA CUP WINNERS: 1958

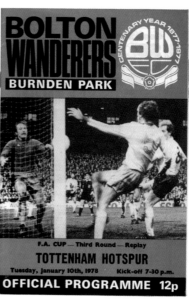

AFC BOURNEMOUTH

FOUNDED: 1899
GROUND: Dean Court
NICKNAME: The Cherries
PREVIOUS NAME: Bournemouth & Boscombe Athletic

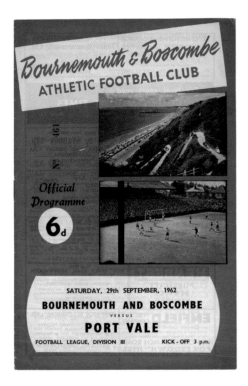

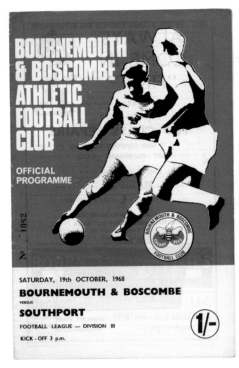

BRADFORD CITY

FOUNDED: 1903
GROUND: Valley Parade
NICKNAME: The Bantams

B R A D F O R D

CITY

Association Football Club (1908) Ltd.

Directors :

Mr. S. Heginbotham (Chairman), Mr. M. G. F. Dickens (Vice–Chairman)
Mr. G. D. Ide, Mr. H. B. Metcalfe, Mr. E. L. Porter
Hon. Medical Officer : Dr. R. Strachan
Team Manager : Mr. J. Wheeler   Secretary : Mr. J. Mellor

SATURDAY, 7th MARCH, 1970

versus

BRISTOL ROVERS

KICK–OFF 3 p.m.

OFFICIAL PROGRAMME : ONE SHILLING

Bradford City

a.f.c

LEAGUE DIVISION THREE
Bradford City
VERSUS
Colchester U.
Saturday, 7th January, 1978
Kick-off 3.00 p.m.
Official Programme 15p

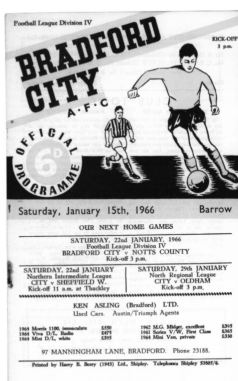

Football League Division IV

KICK-OFF
3 p.m.

BRADFORD CITY A·F·C

OFFICIAL 6D PROGRAMME

Saturday, January 15th, 1966   Barrow

OUR NEXT HOME GAMES

SATURDAY, 22nd JANUARY, 1966
Football League Division IV
BRADFORD CITY v NOTTS COUNTY
Kick-off 3 p.m.

SATURDAY, 22nd JANUARY	SATURDAY, 29th JANUARY
Northern Intermediate League	North Regional League
CITY v SHEFFIELD W.	CITY v OLDHAM
Kick-off 11 a.m. at Thackley	Kick-off 3 p.m.

KEN ASLING (Bradford) LTD.
Used Cars. Austin/Triumph Agents

1964 Morris 1100, immaculate	£550	1962 M.G. Midget, excellent	£395
1964 Viva D/L, Radio	£475	1961 Series V/W, First Class	£365
1964 Mini D/L, white	£395	1964 Mini Van, private	£330

97 MANNINGHAM LANE, BRADFORD. Phone 23188.

Printed by Harry B. Berry (1943) Ltd., Shipley. Telephone Shipley 53805/6.

Bradford
CITY
v
HARTLEPOOL UNITED
December 2nd, 1978
K.O. 3pm.
F.L. 4th Division

The Parader

OFFICIAL PROGRAMME 20p

BRADFORD PARK AVENUE

FOUNDED: 1907, reformed 1989
GROUND: Park Avenue, Horsfall Stadium
NICKNAME: Avenue

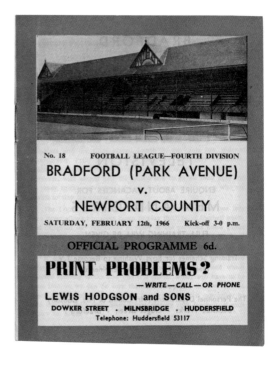

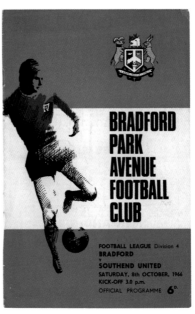

BRENTFORD

FOUNDED: 1889
GROUND: Griffin Park
NICKNAME: The Bees

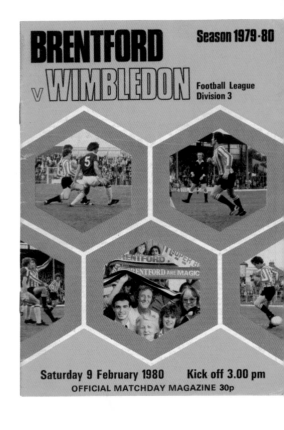

BRENTFORD
v WIMBLEDON

Season 1979-80

Football League
Division 3

Saturday 9 February 1980   Kick off 3.00 pm
OFFICIAL MATCHDAY MAGAZINE 30p

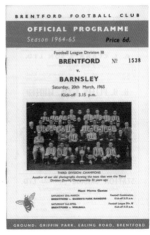

BRIGHTON & HOVE ALBION

FOUNDED: 1900
GROUND: Goldstone Ground
NICKNAME: The Seagulls

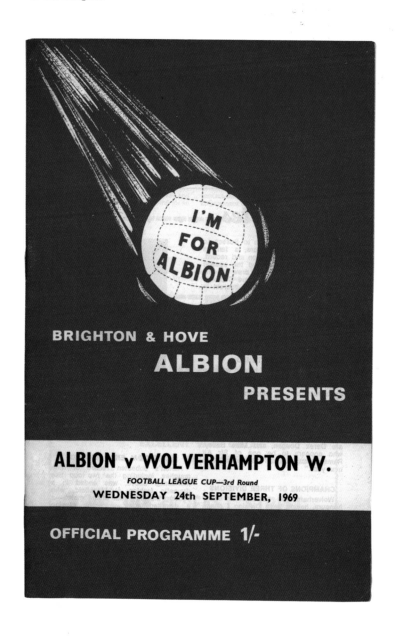

I'M FOR ALBION

BRIGHTON & HOVE
ALBION
PRESENTS

ALBION v WOLVERHAMPTON W.
FOOTBALL LEAGUE CUP—3rd Round
WEDNESDAY 24th SEPTEMBER, 1969

OFFICIAL PROGRAMME 1/-

BRIGHTON & HOVE

ALBION NEWS

ALBION
v.
ROTHERHAM U.
WEDNESDAY
26th APRIL 1972

OFFICIAL PROGRAMME
5p
WITH FOOTBALL LEAGUE REVIEW

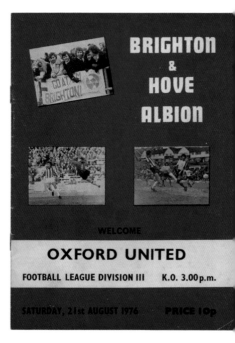

BRIGHTON
&
HOVE
ALBION

WELCOME

OXFORD UNITED

FOOTBALL LEAGUE DIVISION III   K.O. 3.00 p.m.

SATURDAY, 21st AUGUST 1976   PRICE 10p

BRIGHTON & HOVE ALBION

Football League Division 1   Monday, February 4, 1980   Kick-off 7.45 p.m.

ASTON VILLA

SEASON 1979-80   OFFICIAL PROGRAMME 20p

BRISTOL CITY

FOUNDED: 1894
GROUND: Ashton Gate
NICKNAME: The Robins

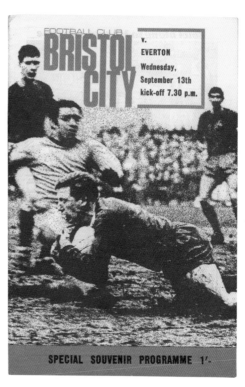

BRISTOL ROVERS

FOUNDED: 1883
GROUND: Eastville, Memorial Stadium
NICKNAME: The Pirates

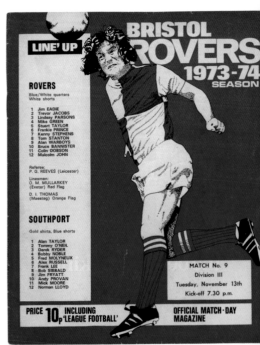

BURNLEY

FOUNDED: 1882
GROUND: Turf Moor
NICKNAME: The Clarets

LEAGUE CHAMPIONS: 1960

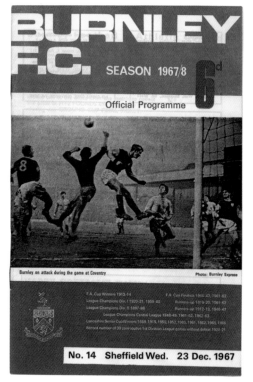

BURY

FOUNDED: 1885
GROUND: Gigg Lane
NICKNAME: The Shakers

CAMBRIDGE UNITED

FOUNDED: 1919
GROUND: Abbey Stadium
NICKNAME: The U's

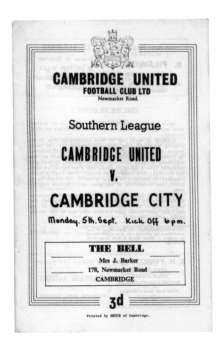

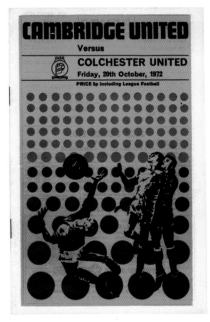

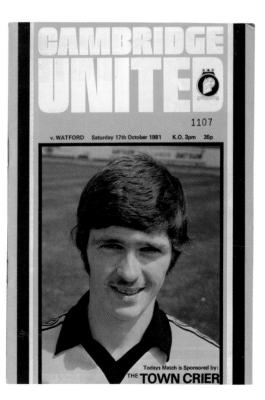

CARDIFF CITY

FOUNDED: 1899
GROUND: Ninian Park
NICKNAME: The Bluebirds

CARLISLE UNITED

FOUNDED: 1904
GROUND: Brunton Park
NICKNAME: The Cumbrians, Blues

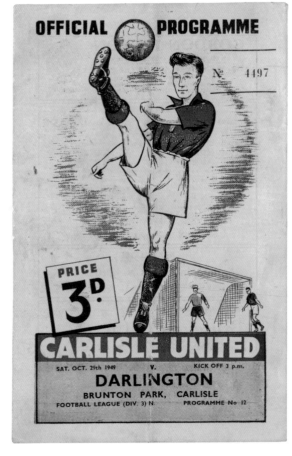

CHARLTON ATHLETIC

FOUNDED: 1905
GROUND: The Valley
NICKNAME: The Addicks

FA CUP WINNERS: 1947

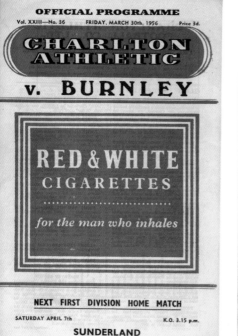

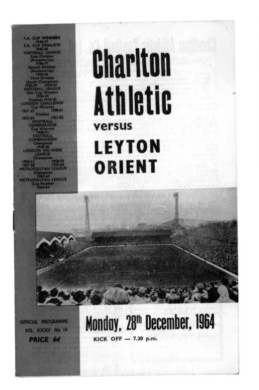

Charlton
Athletic
versus
LEYTON
ORIENT

OFFICIAL PROGRAMME
VOL. XXXII No. 16
PRICE 6d

Monday, 28th December, 1964

KICK OFF — 7.30 p.m.

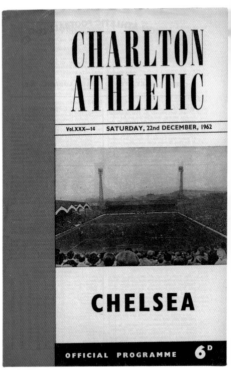

CHARLTON
ATHLETIC

Vol.XXX—14   SATURDAY, 22nd December, 1962

CHELSEA

OFFICIAL PROGRAMME   6D

SUNDERLAND
Saturday, 11th November 1978
Kick-off: 3.00 p.m.
Price 20p

CHELSEA

FOUNDED: 1905
GROUND: Stamford Bridge
NICKNAME: The Blues

LEAGUE CHAMPIONS: 1955
FA CUP WINNERS: 1970
EUROPEAN CUP WINNERS' CUP WINNERS: 1971

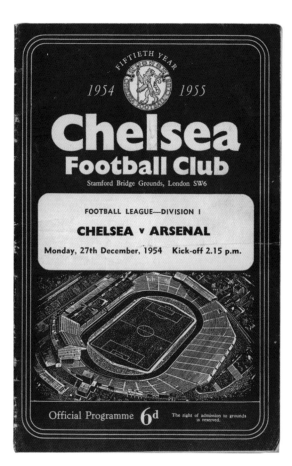

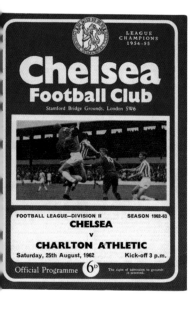

Winners of European Cup-Winners' Cup 1971

Chelsea

Football League Division One—Season 1971/72
Saturday, 2nd October
WOLVERHAMPTON WANDERERS
Kick-off 3 p.m.

OFFICIAL PROGRAMME 5P

Season 1972-73

CHELSEA

FOOTBALL LEAGUE CUP — SEMI-FINAL, FIRST LEG
· Wednesday 6 December
Norwich City
Kick off 7.45 pm

OFFICIAL PROGRAMME 5p

FOOTBALL LEAGUE DIVISION ONE

Season 1973-74

CHELSEA

Friday 26 October

Norwich City

Kick-off 7.45 pm

OFFICIAL PROGRAMME 5p

Official Programme 15p

CFC

London and Manchester Assurance

Chelsea v Nott'm Forest

FOOTBALL LEAGUE DIVISION TWO/SEASON 76/77/SATURDAY APRIL 16th, 1977/KICK-OFF 3 pm.

CHESTER CITY

FOUNDED: 1884
GROUND: Sealand Road
NICKNAME: The Seals, Blues
PREVIOUS NAME: Chester

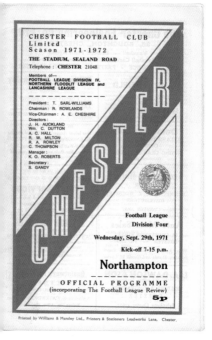

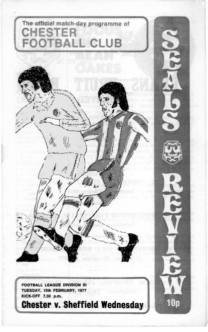

CHESTERFIELD

FOUNDED: 1866
GROUND: Saltergate
NICKNAME: The Spireites

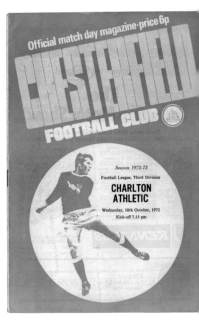

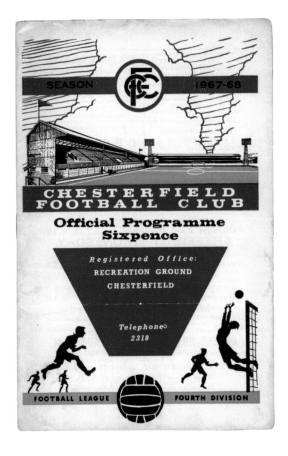

COLCHESTER UNITED

FOUNDED: 1937
GROUND: Layer Road
NICKNAME: The U's

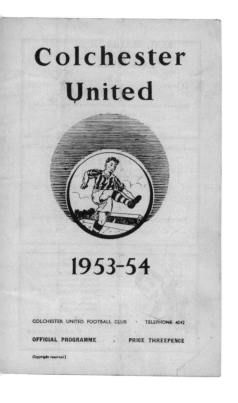

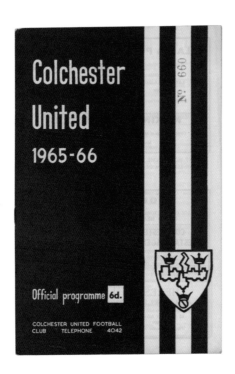

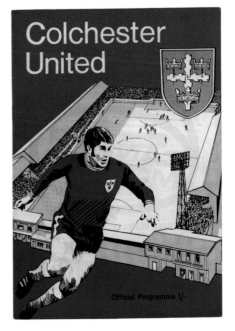

COVENTRY CITY

FOUNDED: 1883
GROUND: Highfield Road
NICKNAME: The Sky Blues

FA CUP WINNERS: 1987

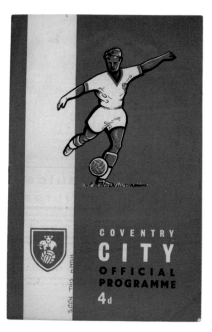

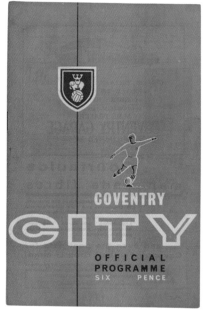

SKY BLUE
MARK 2

SKY BLUE, THE OFFICIAL MAGAZINE OF THE COVENTRY CITY FOOTBALL CLUB LIMITED / VOLUME ONE / NUMBER THIRTEEN

Your 'Sky Blue' host for today's Football League, Division One game is Brian Jukey. The match: **Sky Blues v Manchester City.** The place: Highfield Road. The date: 7th November 1970. Kick-off: 3.15 pm. Manchester City have won almost everything since their return from the Second Division. They have won the League Championship, F.A. Cup and Cup Winners Cup, and with Joe Mercer and Malcolm Allison at the managerial reins and players of the calibre of Colin Bell, Francis Lee and Tony Book, what more can we say!

PRESIDENT: Dr CUTHBERT K. N. BARDSLEY, C.B.E., M.A. (LORD BISHOP OF COVENTRY), CHAIRMAN DERRICK H. ROBINS VICE-CHAIRMAN J. R. MEAD, J.P., F.C.A. DIRECTORS PETER D. H. ROBINS, MICHAEL FRENCH, F.C.A., THOMAS SERGEANT, F.R.C.S. MEDICAL OFFICER Dr T. BAIRD, GENERAL MANAGER NOEL CANTWELL, SECRETARY EDDIE PLUMLEY, CHEF & CATERING MANAGER FRANK HUNT, MAITRE d'HOTEL GIOVANNI, ADVERTISING CONSULTANT PETER STURTZ, MAGAZINE EDITOR JOHN ELVIN

COVENTRY CITY v MANCHESTER CITY / 7th NOVEMBER 1970 / 'SKY BLUE' OFFICIAL MATCHDAY MAGAZINE **2**/ (10 N.P.)

SKY BLUE
MARK 2

SKY BLUE, THE OFFICIAL MAGAZINE OF THE COVENTRY CITY FOOTBALL CLUB LIMITED / VOLUME ONE / NUMBER FOURTEEN

Your 'Sky Blue' host for today's Football League Division One game is Mick Coop. The match: **Sky Blues v Crystal Palace.** The place: Highfield Road. The date: 21st November 1970. Kick-off: 3.15 pm. Palace visit us today poised on the brink of a strong challenge for the First Division Championship. Today's 'Sky Blue' Caveman is Liverpool's brilliant 'keeper, Ray Clemence who made sure we came away with only one point from our 0-0 draw at Anfield last Saturday. In today's magazine: 'Crystal Palace, Focus on Mick Coop and Junior Sky Blues.

PRESIDENT: Dr CUTHBERT K. N. BARDSLEY, C.B.E., M.A. (LORD BISHOP OF COVENTRY), CHAIRMAN DERRICK H. ROBINS VICE-CHAIRMAN J. R. MEAD, J.P., F.C.A. DIRECTORS PETER D. H. ROBINS, MICHAEL FRENCH, F.C.A., THOMAS SERGEANT, F.R.C.S. MEDICAL OFFICER Dr T. BAIRD, GENERAL MANAGER NOEL CANTWELL, SECRETARY EDDIE PLUMLEY, CHEF & CATERING MANAGER FRANK HUNT, MAITRE d'HOTEL GIOVANNI, ADVERTISING CONSULTANT PETER STURTZ, MAGAZINE EDITOR JOHN ELVIN

COVENTRY CITY v CRYSTAL PALACE / 21st NOVEMBER 1970 / 'SKY BLUE' OFFICIAL MATCHDAY MAGAZINE **2**/ (10 N.P.)

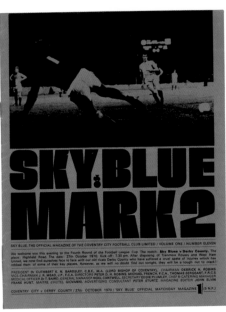

SKY BLUE
MARK 2

SKY BLUE, THE OFFICIAL MAGAZINE OF THE COVENTRY CITY FOOTBALL CLUB LIMITED / VOLUME ONE / NUMBER ELEVEN

We welcome you this evening to the Fourth Round of the Football League Cup. The match: **Sky Blues v Derby County.** The place: Highfield Road. The date: 27th October 1970. Kick-off: 7.30 pm. After disposing of Tranmere Rovers and West Ham United, we now find ourselves face to face with our old rivals Derby County who have suffered a cruel spate of injuries which has robbed them of some of their key players. However, as we will no doubt find out tonight, they will be a tough nut to crack!

PRESIDENT: Dr CUTHBERT K. N. BARDSLEY, C.B.E., M.A. (LORD BISHOP OF COVENTRY), CHAIRMAN DERRICK H. ROBINS VICE-CHAIRMAN J. R. MEAD, J.P., F.C.A. DIRECTORS PETER D. H. ROBINS, MICHAEL FRENCH, F.C.A., THOMAS SERGEANT, F.R.C.S. MEDICAL OFFICER Dr T. BAIRD, GENERAL MANAGER NOEL CANTWELL, SECRETARY EDDIE PLUMLEY, CHEF & CATERING MANAGER FRANK HUNT, MAITRE d'HOTEL GIOVANNI, ADVERTISING CONSULTANT PETER STURTZ, MAGAZINE EDITOR JOHN ELVIN

COVENTRY CITY v DERBY COUNTY / 27th OCTOBER 1970 / 'SKY BLUE' OFFICIAL MATCHDAY MAGAZINE **1**/ (5 N.P.)

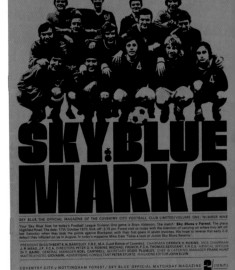

SKY BLUE
MARK 2

SKY BLUE, THE OFFICIAL MAGAZINE OF THE COVENTRY CITY FOOTBALL CLUB LIMITED / VOLUME ONE / NUMBER NINE

Your 'Sky Blue' host for today's Football League Division One game is Brian Alderson. The match: **Sky Blues v Forest.** The place: Highfield Road. The date: 17th October 1970. Kick-off: 3.15 pm. Forest visit us today with the intention of carrying on where they left off last Saturday when they took the points against Blackpool, with their first goals in seven matches. We hope to reverse that early 2-0 defeat they reflected on us in August. In today's magazine Mike Oale 'Takes a look at Junior Sky Blues Seventy'.

PRESIDENT: Dr CUTHBERT K. N. BARDSLEY, C.B.E., M.A. (Lord Bishop of Coventry), CHAIRMAN DERRICK H. ROBINS, VICE-CHAIRMAN J. R. MEAD, J.P., F.C.A. DIRECTORS PETER D. H. ROBINS, MICHAEL FRENCH, F.C.A., THOMAS SERGEANT, F.R.C.S. MEDICAL OFFICER Dr T. BAIRD, GENERAL MANAGER NOEL CANTWELL, SECRETARY EDDIE PLUMLEY, CHEF & CATERING MANAGER FRANK HUNT, MAITRE d'HOTEL GIOVANNI, ADVERTISING CONSULTANT PETER STURTZ, MAGAZINE EDITOR JOHN ELVIN

COVENTRY CITY v NOTTINGHAM FOREST / 'SKY BLUE' OFFICIAL MATCHDAY MAGAZINE **2**/ (10 N.P.)

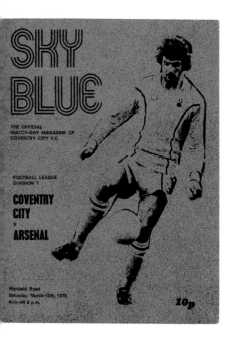

SKY BLUE

THE OFFICIAL
MATCH-DAY MAGAZINE OF
COVENTRY CITY F.C.

FOOTBALL LEAGUE
DIVISION 1

**COVENTRY
CITY**

v

ARSENAL

Highfield Road
Saturday, March 13th, 1976
Kick-off 3 p.m.

10p

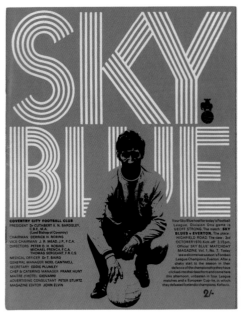

**SKY
BLUE**

COVENTRY CITY FOOTBALL CLUB
PRESIDENT Dr CUTHBERT K. N. BARDSLEY,
C.B.E., M.A.
(Lord Bishop of Coventry)
CHAIRMAN DERRICK H. ROBINS
VICE-CHAIRMAN J. R. MEAD, J.P., F.C.A.
DIRECTORS PETER D. H. ROBINS
MICHAEL FRENCH, F.C.A.
THOMAS SERGEANT, F.R.C.S.
MEDICAL OFFICER Dr T. BAIRD
GENERAL MANAGER NOEL CANTWELL
SECRETARY EDDIE PLUMLEY
CHEF & CATERING MANAGER FRANK HUNT
MAITRE d'HOTEL GIOVANNI
ADVERTISING CONSULTANT PETER STURTZ
MAGAZINE EDITOR JOHN ELVIN

Your Sky Blue host for today's Football
League. Division One game is
GEOFF STRONG. The match : **SKY
BLUES v EVERTON.** The place :
HIGHFIELD ROAD. The date : 3rd
OCTOBER 1970. Kick-off 3.15pm.
Official 'SKY BLUE' MATCHDAY
MAGAZINE, Vol. 1, No. 7. Today
we welcome last season's Football
League Champions, Everton. After a
shaky start to the season in their
defence of the championship they have
clicked into their best form and come here
this afternoon, unbeaten in four League
matches and a European Cup-tie, in which
they defeated Icelandic champions, Keflavic.

2/-

FIRST DIVISION · TUESDAY 24th AUGUST 1976 · K.O. 7.30 P.M.

SKY BLUES

**MANCHESTER
UNITED**

OFFICIAL MATCHDAY MAGAZINE OF COVENTRY CITY F.C. **15p**

CREWE ALEXANDRA

FOUNDED: 1877
GROUND: Gresty Road
NICKNAME: The Railwaymen

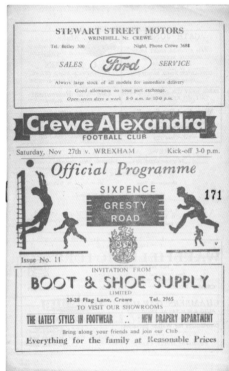

CRYSTAL PALACE

FOUNDED: 1905
GROUND: Selhurst Park
NICKNAME: The Eagles

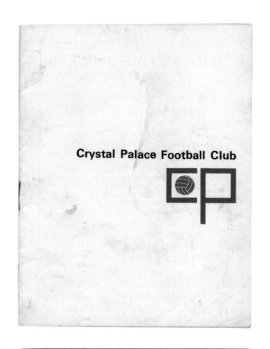

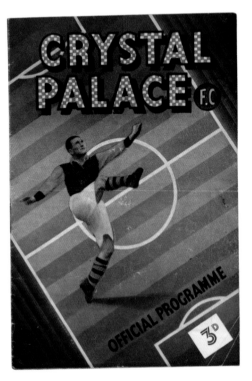

DARLINGTON

FOUNDED: 1883
GROUND: Feethams
NICKNAME: The Quakers

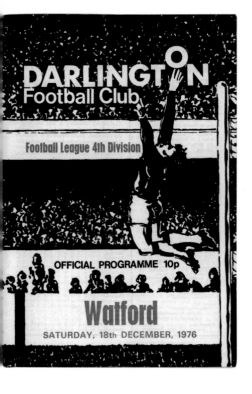

DERBY COUNTY

FOUNDED: 1884
GROUND: Baseball Ground
NICKNAME: The Rams

LEAGUE CHAMPIONS: 1972, 1975
FA CUP WINNERS: 1946

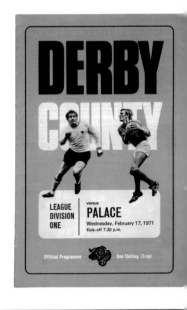

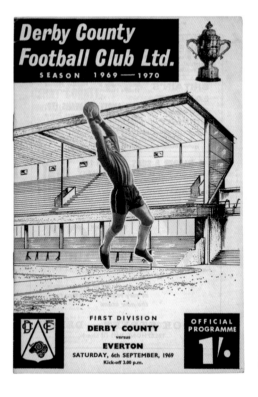

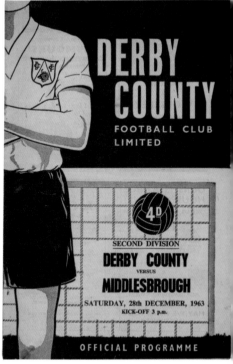

Official NEWSPAPER/PROGRAMME of DERBY COUNTY F.C.

RAM

**Vol 8, Number 12
Mon. Jan. 1, 1979
Ipswich Town**

20p

Derby's Eire International mid-field star Gerry Daly with his attractive wife Sheila

DONCASTER ROVERS

FOUNDED: 1879
GROUND: Belle Vue
NICKNAME: Rovers

EVERTON

FOUNDED: 1878
GROUND: Goodison Park
NICKNAME: The Toffees

LEAGUE CHAMPIONS: 1963, 1970, 1985, 1987
FA CUP WINNERS: 1966, 1984
EUROPEAN CUP WINNERS' CUP WINNERS: 1985

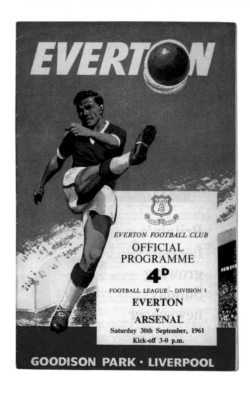

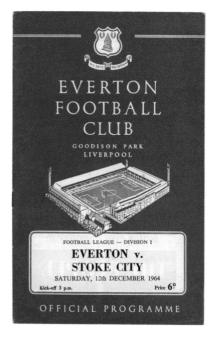

EXETER CITY

FOUNDED: 1904
GROUND: St James' Park
NICKNAME: The Grecians

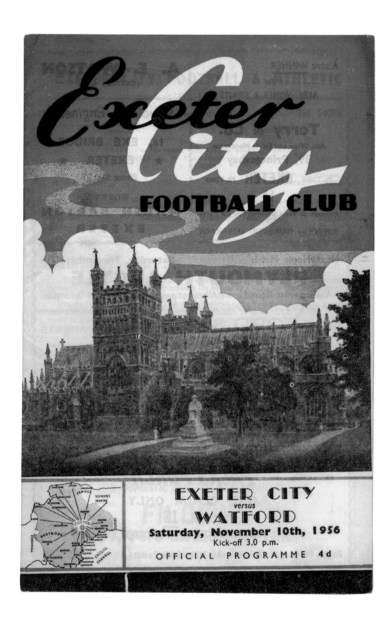

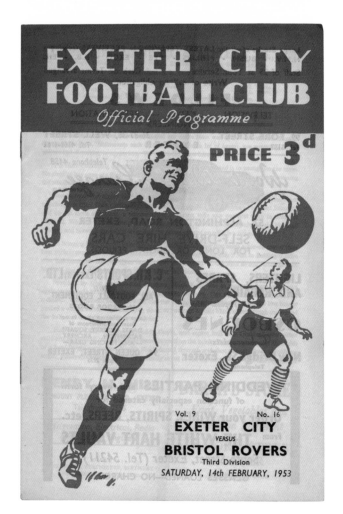

EXETER CITY
FOOTBALL CLUB
Official Programme

PRICE 3d

Vol. 9   No. 16
EXETER CITY
VERSUS
BRISTOL ROVERS
Third Division
SATURDAY, 14th FEBRUARY, 1953

Official Programme 5p

EXETER
CITY
FOOTBALL
CLUB

City

v STOCKPORT COUNTY
ST. JAMES' PARK, EXETER

Saturday
23rd October, 1971
Kick-off 3 p.m.

Fourth Division

FULHAM

FOUNDED: 1880
GROUND: Craven Cottage
NICKNAME: The Cottagers

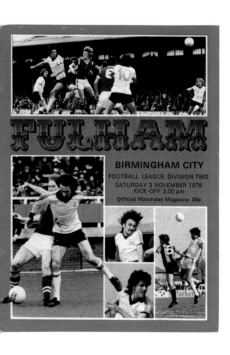

BIRMINGHAM CITY
FOOTBALL LEAGUE DIVISION TWO
SATURDAY 3 NOVEMBER 1979
KICK-OFF 3.00 pm
Official Matchday Magazine 25p

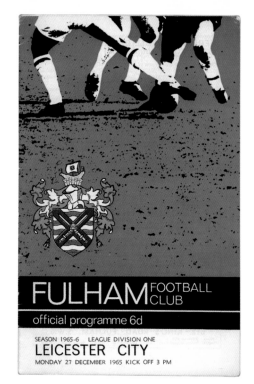

FULHAM FOOTBALL CLUB
official programme 6d

SEASON 1965-6   LEAGUE DIVISION ONE
LEICESTER CITY
MONDAY 27 DECEMBER 1965 KICK OFF 3 PM

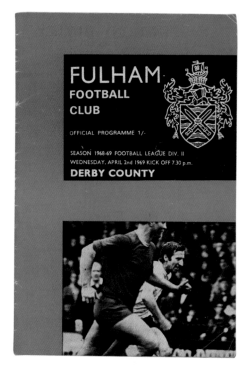

FULHAM
FOOTBALL
CLUB

OFFICIAL PROGRAMME 1/-

SEASON 1968-69 FOOTBALL LEAGUE DIV. II
WEDNESDAY, APRIL 2nd 1969 KICK OFF 7.30 p.m.
DERBY COUNTY

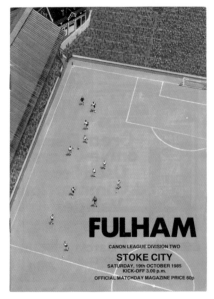

GATESHEAD

FOUNDED: 1930, reformed 1977
GROUND: Redheugh Park, Gateshead International Stadium
NICKNAME: The Tynesiders

GILLINGHAM

FOUNDED: 1893
GROUND: Priestfield Stadium
NICKNAME: The Gills

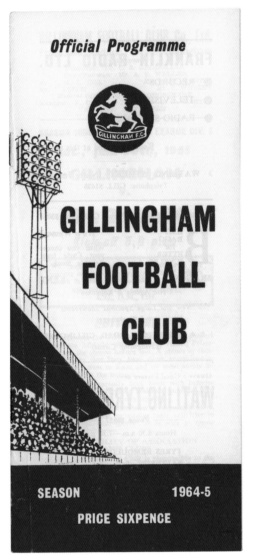

GRIMSBY TOWN

FOUNDED: 1878
GROUND: Blundell Park
NICKNAME: The Mariners

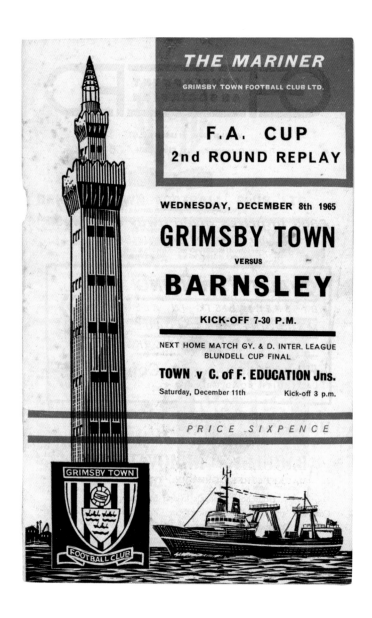

HALIFAX TOWN

FOUNDED: 1911
GROUND: The Shay
NICKNAME: The Shaymen

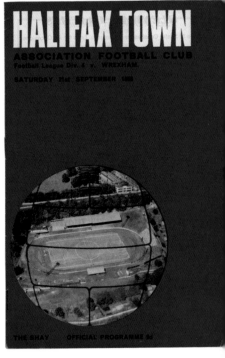

HARTLEPOOL

FOUNDED: 1908
GROUND: Victoria Ground
NICKNAME: Pool
PREVIOUS NAME: Hartlepools United

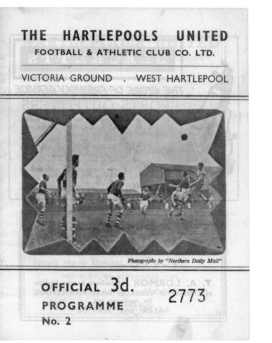

HEREFORD UNITED

FOUNDED: 1924
GROUND: Edgar Street
NICKNAME: The Bulls

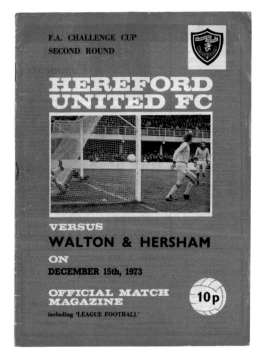

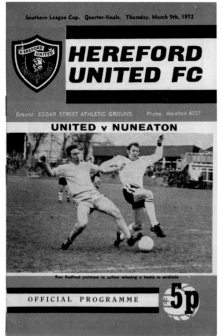

HUDDERSFIELD TOWN

FOUNDED: 1908
GROUND: Leeds Road
NICKNAME: The Terriers

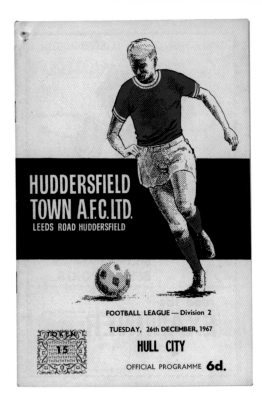

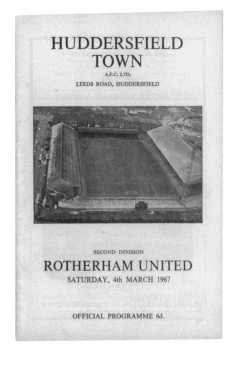

HULL CITY

FOUNDED: 1904
GROUND: Boothferry Park
NICKNAME: The Tigers

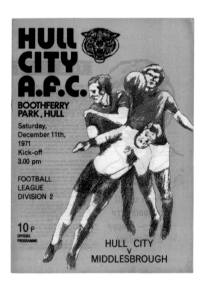

IPSWICH TOWN

FOUNDED: 1878
GROUND: Portman Road
NICKNAME: The Blues, Town

LEAGUE CHAMPIONS: 1962
FA CUP WINNERS: 1978
UEFA CUP WINNERS: 1981

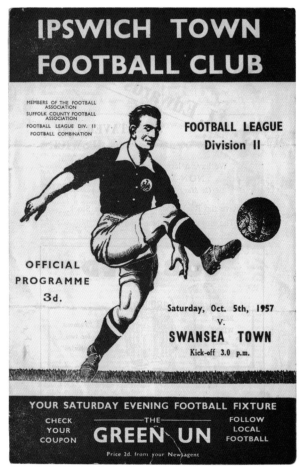

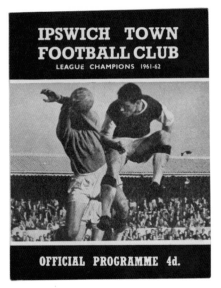

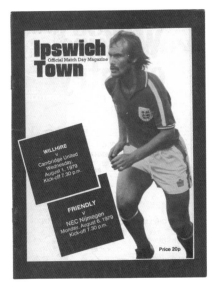

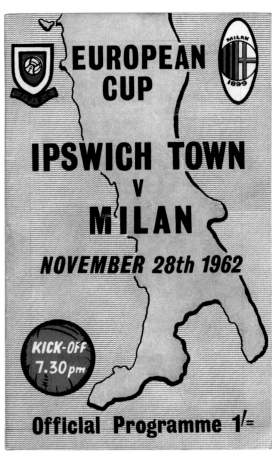

LEEDS UNITED

FOUNDED: 1919
GROUND: Elland Road
NICKNAME: The Peacocks

LEAGUE CHAMPIONS: 1969, 1974, 1992
FA CUP WINNERS: 1972
LEAGUE CUP WINNERS: 1968
UEFA CUP WINNERS: 1971

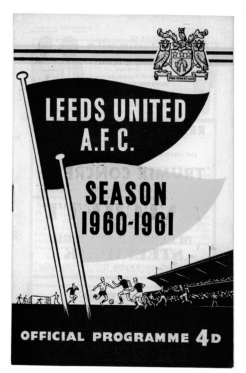

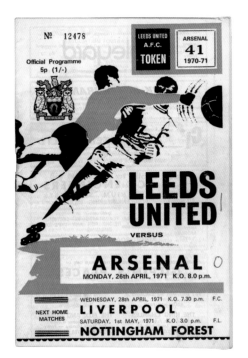

№ 12478

Official Programme
5p (1/-)

LEEDS UNITED
A.F.C.
TOKEN

ARSENAL
41
1970-71

LEEDS
UNITED

VERSUS

ARSENAL O

MONDAY, 26th APRIL, 1971 K.O. 8.0 p.m.

NEXT HOME
MATCHES

WEDNESDAY, 28th APRIL, 1971 K.O. 7.30 p.m. F.C.

LIVERPOOL

SATURDAY, 1st MAY, 1971 K.O. 3.0 p.m. F.L.

NOTTINGHAM FOREST

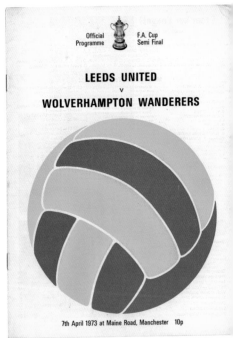

Official
Programme

F.A. Cup
Semi Final

LEEDS UNITED
v
WOLVERHAMPTON WANDERERS

7th April 1973 at Maine Road, Manchester 10p

LEICESTER CITY

FOUNDED: 1884
GROUND: Filbert Street
NICKNAME: The Foxes

LEAGUE CUP WINNERS: 1964

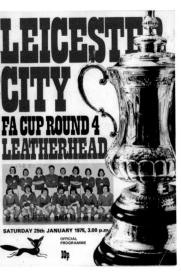

LEYTON ORIENT

FOUNDED: 1881
GROUND: Brisbane Road
NICKNAME: The O's
PREVIOUS NAME: Orient

LINCOLN CITY

FOUNDED: 1884
GROUND: Sincil Bank
NICKNAME: The Imps

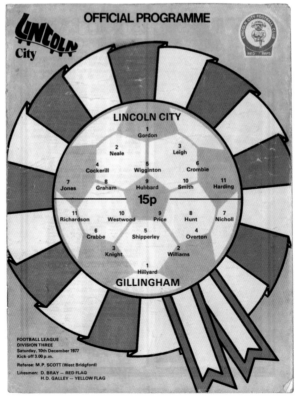

LIVERPOOL

FOUNDED: 1892
GROUND: Anfield
NICKNAME: The Reds

LEAGUE CHAMPIONS: 1947, 1964, 1966, 1973, 1976, 1977, 1979, 1980, 1982, 1983, 1984, 1986, 1988, 1990
FA CUP WINNERS: 1965, 1974, 1986, 1989, 1992
LEAGUE CUP WINNERS: 1981, 1982, 1983, 1984
EUROPEAN CUP WINNERS: 1977, 1978, 1981, 1984
UEFA CUP WINNERS: 1973, 1976

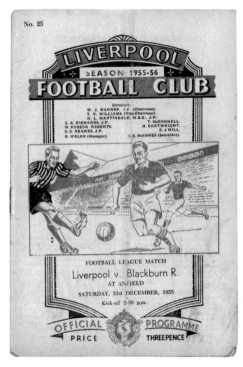

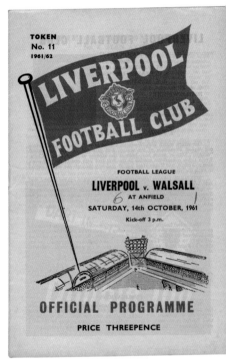

LIVERPOOL

LEAGUE
DIVISION 1

Saturday
10th September
1977

Kick-off
3.00 p.m.

LIVERPOOL
versus
COVENTRY
CITY

CHAIRMAN
John W. Smith, J.P.

VICE-CHAIRMAN
J. T. Cross

DIRECTORS:
H. Cartwright
S. C. Reakes, J.P.
C. J. Hill
E. A. F. Sawyer
W. D. Corkish,
F.C.A.

TEAM MANAGER
Bob Paisley

GENERAL
SECRETARY
Peter Robinson

WHAT'S INSIDE
- World Cup comes to Anfield
- Bob Paisley's Team Talk
- Spotlight on Sky Blues
- Action pictures
- Liverpool landmarks
- New boys on mark
- Cally's big date

THE ANFIELD REVIEW   **15p**

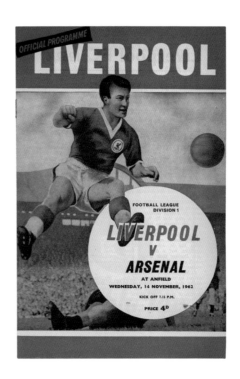

OFFICIAL PROGRAMME

LIVERPOOL

FOOTBALL LEAGUE
DIVISION 1

LIVERPOOL v *ARSENAL*

AT ANFIELD
WEDNESDAY, 14 NOVEMBER, 1962

KICK OFF 7.15 P.M.

PRICE 4D

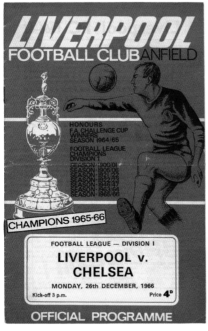

LIVERPOOL
FOOTBALL CLUB ANFIELD

HONOURS
F.A. CHALLENGE CUP
WINNERS
SEASON 1964/65
FOOTBALL LEAGUE
CHAMPIONS
DIVISION 1
SEASON 1900-01
SEASON 1905-06
SEASON 1921-22
SEASON 1922-23
SEASON 1946-47
SEASON 1963-64
SEASON 1965-66

CHAMPIONS 1965-66

FOOTBALL LEAGUE — DIVISION I
LIVERPOOL v. CHELSEA

MONDAY, 26th DECEMBER, 1966

Kick-off 3 p.m.   Price 4D

OFFICIAL PROGRAMME

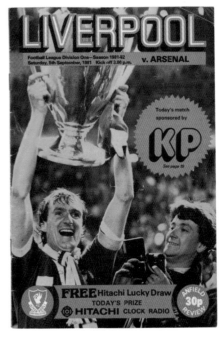

LIVERPOOL
v. ARSENAL

Football League Division One—Season 1981-82
Saturday, 5th September, 1981   Kick-off 3.00 p.m.

Today's match
sponsored by

KP
See page 19

FREE Hitachi Lucky Draw
TODAY'S PRIZE
HITACHI CLOCK RADIO

ANFIELD
REVIEW
30p

LUTON TOWN

FOUNDED: 1885
GROUND: Kenilworth Road
NICKNAME: The Hatters

LEAGUE CUP WINNERS: 1988

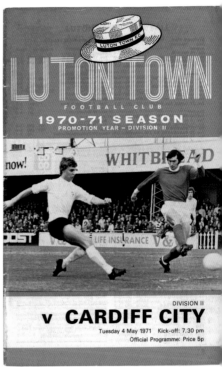

LUTON TOWN

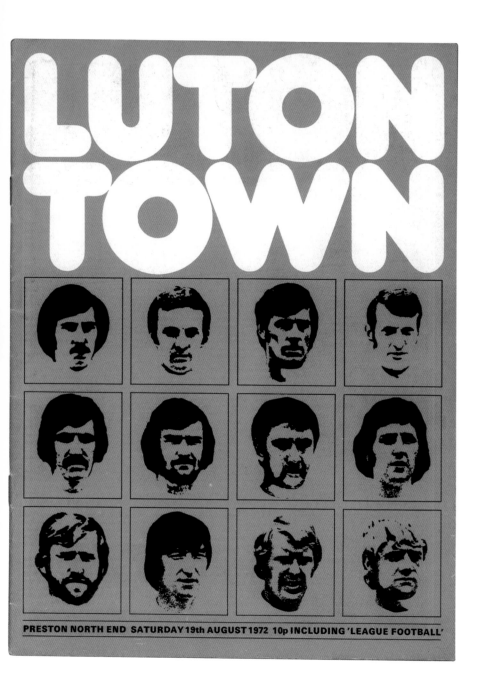

PRESTON NORTH END SATURDAY 19th AUGUST 1972 10p INCLUDING 'LEAGUE FOOTBALL'

MAIDSTONE UNITED

FOUNDED: 1897
GROUND: London Road
NICKNAME: The Stones

MANCHESTER CITY

FOUNDED: 1887
GROUND: Maine Road
NICKNAME: City

LEAGUE CHAMPIONS: 1968
FA CUP WINNERS: 1956, 1969
LEAGUE CUP WINNERS: 1970, 1976
EUROPEAN CUP WINNERS' CUP WINNERS: 1970

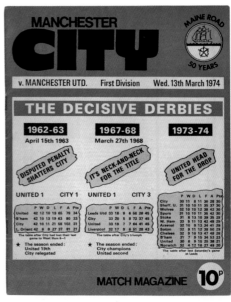

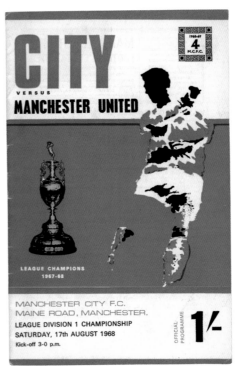

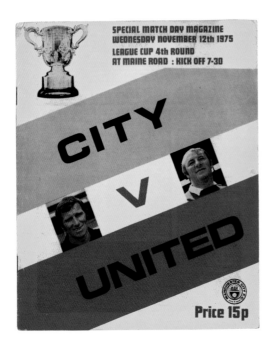

SPECIAL MATCH DAY MAGAZINE
WEDNESDAY NOVEMBER 12th 1975
LEAGUE CUP 4th ROUND
AT MAINE ROAD : KICK OFF 7-30

CITY
v
UNITED

Price 15p

CITY LEAGUE CHAMPIONS

WEDNESDAY
OCTOBER 30th 1968
Kick-off 7-30 p.m.

VERSUS
A.F.C. AJAX (Amsterdam)

MANCHESTER CITY FOOTBALL CLUB LTD.
Challenge Match
OFFICIAL PROGRAMME ONE SHILLING

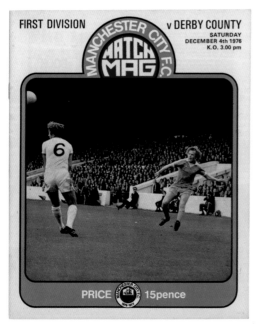

FIRST DIVISION v DERBY COUNTY
SATURDAY
DECEMBER 4th 1976
K.O. 3.00 pm

PRICE 15pence

**MANCHESTER CITY
FOOTBALL CLUB**

OFFICIAL
PROGRAMME 5p.

CITY v NORWICH CITY
Saturday, 19th August 1972 Kick-off 3-00 p.m.

MANCHESTER UNITED

FOUNDED: 1878
GROUND: Old Trafford
NICKNAME: The Red Devils

LEAGUE CHAMPIONS: 1952, 1956, 1957, 1965, 1967
FA CUP WINNERS: 1948, 1963, 1977, 1983, 1985, 1990
LEAGUE CUP WINNERS: 1992
EUROPEAN CUP WINNERS: 1968
EUROPEAN CUP WINNERS' CUP WINNERS: 1992

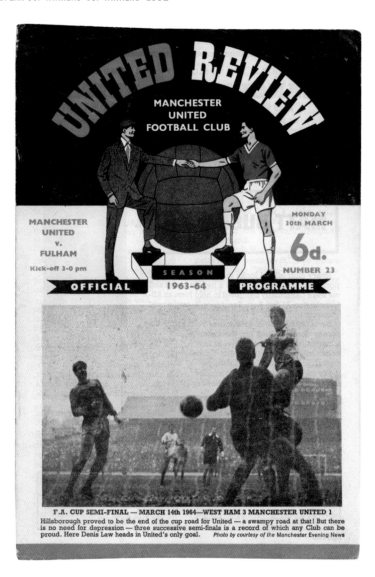

F.A. CUP SEMI-FINAL — MARCH 14th 1964—WEST HAM 3 MANCHESTER UNITED 1
Hillsborough proved to be the end of the cup road for United — a swampy road at that! But there is no need for depression — three successive semi-finals is a record of which any Club can be proud. Here Denis Law heads in United's only goal.   *Photo by courtesy of the Manchester Evening News*

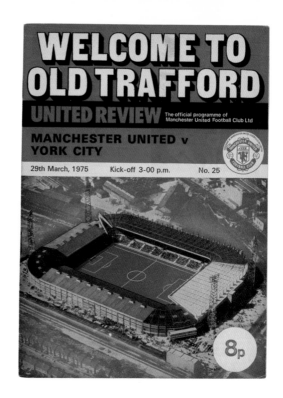

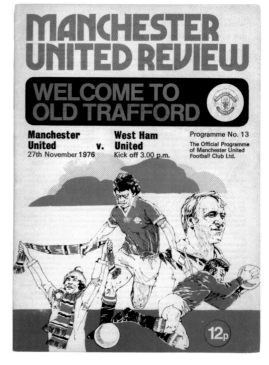

EUROPEAN/SOUTH AMERICAN CUP 1968

No. 9

KICK-OFF 7·45 p.m.

MANCHESTER UNITED
OF ENGLAND
VERSUS
ESTUDIANTES
OF ARGENTINA
OCTOBER 16 1968

price 1/-

UNITED REVIEW

THE OFFICIAL PROGRAMME OF MANCHESTER UNITED FOOTBALL CLUB

WINNERS OF THE EUROPEAN CHAMPIONS CUP COMPETITION 1968

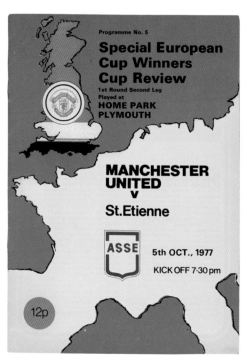

Programme No. 5

Special European Cup Winners Cup Review

1st Round Second Leg
Played at
HOME PARK
PLYMOUTH

MANCHESTER UNITED
v
St.Etienne

ASSE

5th OCT., 1977

KICK OFF 7·30 pm

12p

MANSFIELD TOWN

FOUNDED: 1897
GROUND: Field Mill
NICKNAME: The Stags

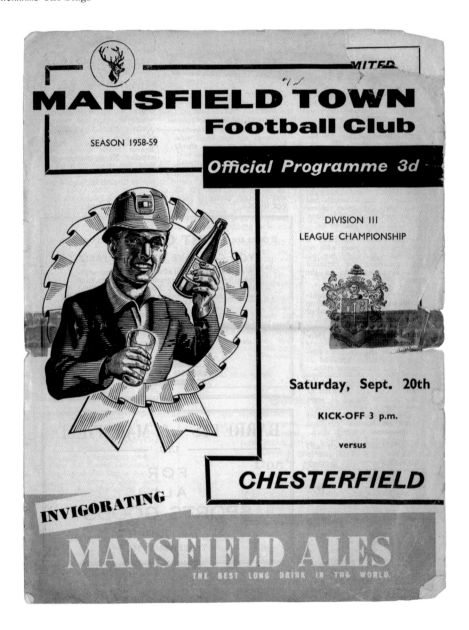

MIDDLESBROUGH

FOUNDED: 1876
GROUND: Ayresome Park
NICKNAME: Boro

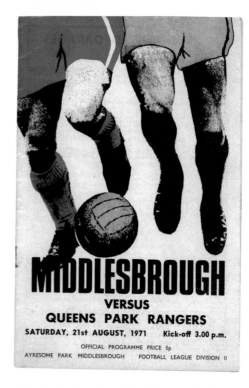

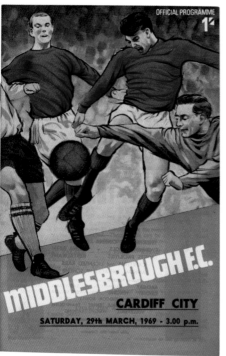

BORO

AYRESOME PARK MIDDLESBROUGH

MATCH MAGAZINE **20**ᴾ

FOOTBALL LEAGUE DIVISION ONE

TOTTENHAM HOTSPUR

Saturday, 3rd November, 1979 Kick-off 3.00 p.m.

Middlesbrough Football Club Ayresome Park

OFFICIAL PROGRAMME   6d

Football League Division II v. SOUTHAMPTON, 6th November, 1965, 3 p.m.

MILLWALL

FOUNDED: 1885
GROUND: The Den
NICKNAME: The Lions

MILLWALL WELCOME

BLACKBURN ROVERS

FOOTBALL LEAGUE
DIVISION TWO
SATURDAY 16 OCTOBER 1976
MATCHDAY MAGAZINE PRICE 12p

MILLWALL FOOTBALL CLUB

BRISTOL CITY

Football League Division II   Saturday 21st November 1970 K.O. 3 p.m.

OFFICIAL CLUB PROGRAMME 1/- (5p)   *Incorporating Football League Review*

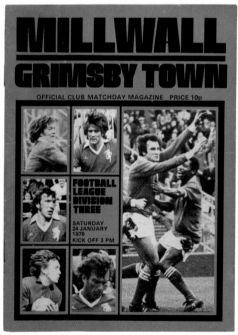

MILLWALL
GRIMSBY TOWN

OFFICIAL CLUB MATCHDAY MAGAZINE   PRICE 10p

FOOTBALL LEAGUE DIVISION THREE

SATURDAY
24 JANUARY
1976
KICK OFF 3 PM

NEW BRIGHTON

FOUNDED: 1921
GROUND: Harrison Park
NICKNAME: The Rakers

NEW BRIGHTON
FOOTBALL CLUB
SEASON 1967-68

VERSUS

RHYL
Wednesday, 23rd August 1967

3d

OFFICIAL PROGRAMME

NEWCASTLE UNITED

FOUNDED: 1882
GROUND: St James' Park
NICKNAME: The Magpies

FA CUP WINNERS: 1951, 1952, 1955
UEFA CUP WINNERS: 1969

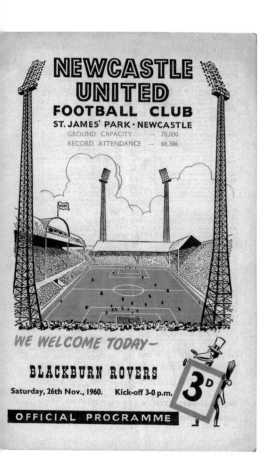

NEWCASTLE UNITED
FOOTBALL CLUB
ST. JAMES' PARK · NEWCASTLE
GROUND CAPACITY — 70,000
RECORD ATTENDANCE — 68,386

WE WELCOME TODAY—

BLACKBURN ROVERS

Saturday, 26th Nov., 1960.   Kick-off 3-0 p.m.

3ᴰ

OFFICIAL PROGRAMME

NEWCASTLE UNITED
FOOTBALL CLUB
ST. JAMES' PARK · NEWCASTLE · ON · TYNE.

OFFICIAL · PROGRAMME
1955 · 1956
PRICE **3**ᴰ

Photo by Bob Edwards

SATURDAY, 3rd DECEMBER   DIVISION 1
NEWCASTLE UTD. v BOLTON WAND.
Kick-off 2.0 p.m.   Programme No. 24

THE BLACK 'n' WHITE

NEWCASTLE UNITED
versus

HENDON

F.A. Cup 3rd Round · Sat., Jan. 5th, 1974 · Kick-off 2.0 p.m.
Vol. 2 No. 19 · Official Match Day Magazine · **10p**

NEWPORT COUNTY

FOUNDED: 1912, reformed 1989
GROUND: Somerton Park
NICKNAME: The Ironsides, Exiles

NORTHAMPTON TOWN

FOUNDED: 1897
GROUND: County Ground
NICKNAME: The Cobblers

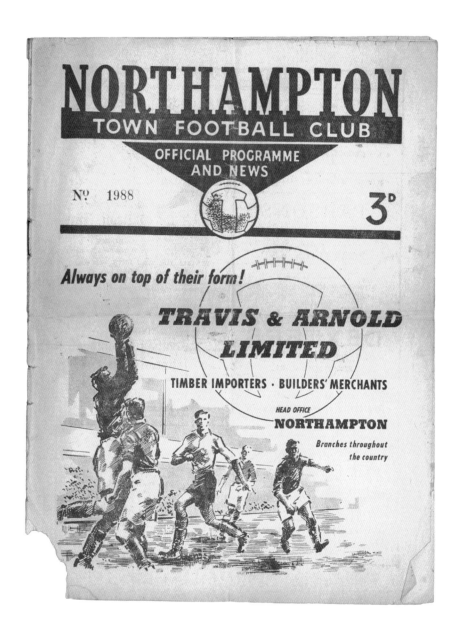

NORTHAMPTON
TOWN FOOTBALL CLUB

OFFICIAL PROGRAMME
AND NEWS

N⁰ 1988

3ᴰ

Always on top of their form!

TRAVIS & ARNOLD
LIMITED

TIMBER IMPORTERS · BUILDERS' MERCHANTS

HEAD OFFICE
NORTHAMPTON

*Branches throughout
the country*

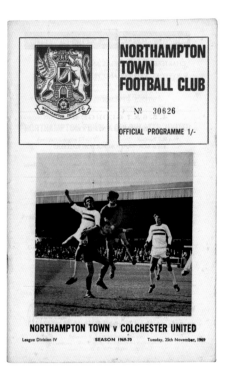

NORTHAMPTON
TOWN
FOOTBALL CLUB

Nº 30626

OFFICIAL PROGRAMME 1/-

NORTHAMPTON TOWN v COLCHESTER UNITED

League Division IV   SEASON 1969-70   Tuesday, 25th November, 1969

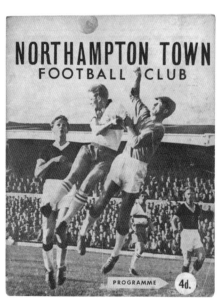

NORTHAMPTON TOWN
FOOTBALL CLUB

PROGRAMME   4d.

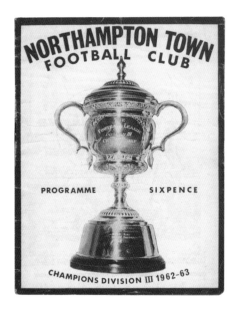

NORTHAMPTON TOWN
FOOTBALL CLUB

PROGRAMME   SIXPENCE

CHAMPIONS DIVISION III 1962-63

NORTHAMPTON TOWN F.C.

OFFICIAL PROGRAMME SIXPENCE

Nº 47076

NORWICH CITY

FOUNDED: 1905
GROUND: Carrow Road
NICKNAME: The Canaries

LEAGUE CUP WINNERS: 1962, 1985

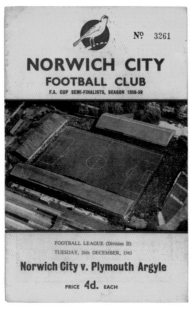

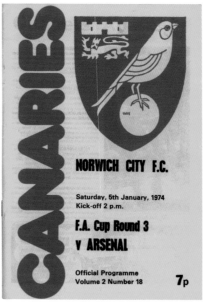

NOTTINGHAM FOREST

FOUNDED: 1865
GROUND: City Ground
NICKNAME: Garibaldi Reds, Forest

LEAGUE CHAMPIONS: 1978
FA CUP WINNERS: 1959
LEAGUE CUP WINNERS: 1978, 1979, 1989, 1990
EUROPEAN CUP WINNERS: 1979, 1980

FOREST

FOREST REVIEW OFFICIAL MATCH-DAY PROGRAMME

EUROPEAN SUPER COMPETITION, 1st LEG

FOREST V. VALENCIA C. de F.

Tuesday, 25th November, 1980

Price 30p

Volume 13
Number 14

NOTTS COUNTY

FOUNDED: 1862
GROUND: Meadow Lane
NICKNAME: The Magpies

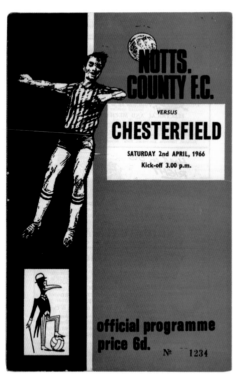

OLDHAM ATHLETIC

FOUNDED: 1895
GROUND: Boundary Park
NICKNAME: The Latics

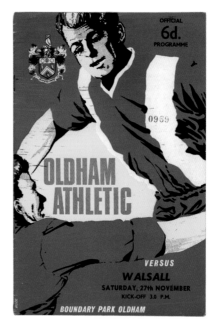

OXFORD UNITED

FOUNDED: 1893
GROUND: Manor Ground
NICKNAME: The U's
PREVIOUS NAME: Headington United

LEAGUE CUP WINNERS: 1986

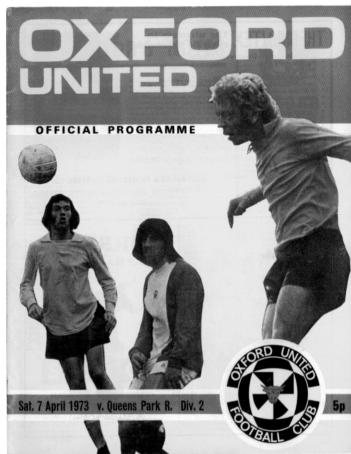

PETERBOROUGH UNITED

FOUNDED: 1923, reformed 1934
GROUND: London Road
NICKNAME: The Posh

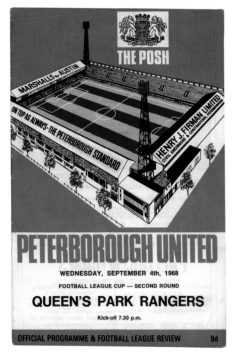

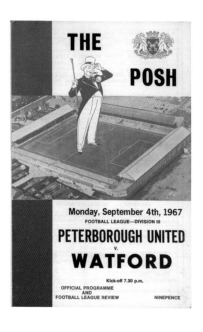

PLYMOUTH ARGYLE

FOUNDED: 1886
GROUND: Home Park
NICKNAME: The Pilgrims

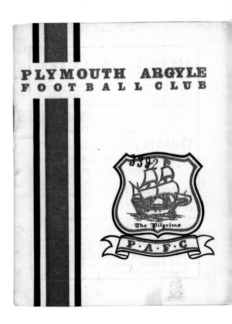

PORTSMOUTH

FOUNDED: 1898
GROUND: Fratton Park
NICKNAME: Pompey

LEAGUE CHAMPIONS: 1949, 1950

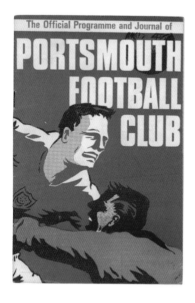

PORT VALE

FOUNDED: 1876
GROUND: Vale Park
NICKNAME: The Valiants

PRESTON NORTH END

FOUNDED: 1880
GROUND: Deepdale
NICKNAME: The Lilywhites

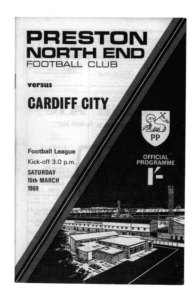

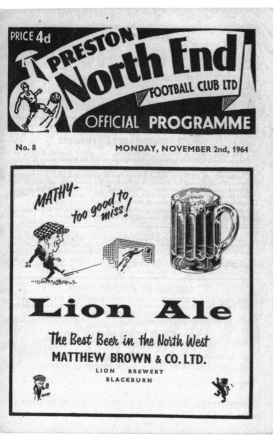

QUEEN'S PARK RANGERS

FOUNDED: 1885
GROUND: Loftus Road
NICKNAME: Rangers, Super Hoops

LEAGUE CUP WINNERS: 1967

QUEEN'S PARK RANGERS

official programme **6**d

F.A. CUP Round 3
SHREWSBURY T.

SATURDAY 22 JANUARY 1966
Kick-off 3.00 p.m.

Club notes BY RANGER

THIS IS IT! The Third Round of the F.A. Cup, with all the trimmings of excitement and glamour, is with us again and with it we welcome another chance to see Rangers through to the next stage of the Competition. It is a long time since we had a really good Cup run. Rangers have not been in the Fourth Round since season 1947/48 and, by our reckoning, the day is long overdue for another. Back in 1948 Rangers got to the 6th Round before going out to Derby County. Here's hoping that this afternoon's match extends our impressive unbeaten run of 13 matches and puts us in line for a plumb draw in the Fourth Round. Next week we return to the important business of the Third Division and stage an attractive home game against

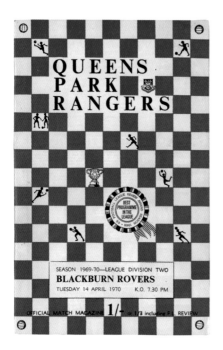

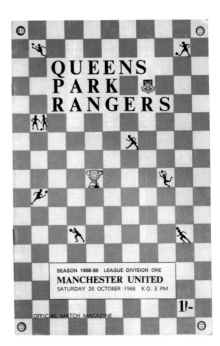

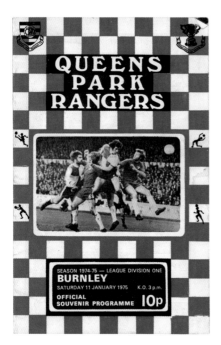

READING

FOUNDED: 1871
GROUND: Elm Park
NICKNAME: The Biscuitmen, Royals

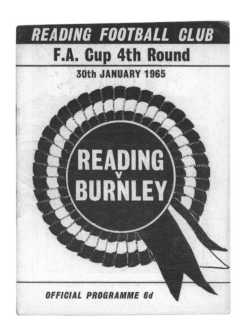

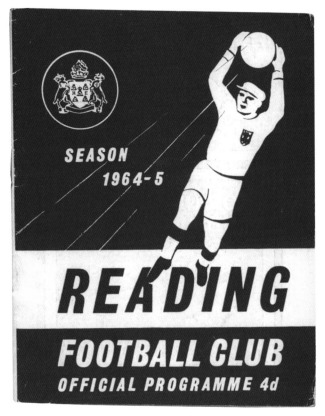

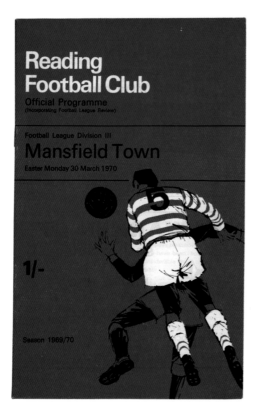

Reading Football Club

Official Programme
(Incorporating Football League Review)

Football League Division III

Mansfield Town

Easter Monday 30 March 1970

1/-

Season 1969/70

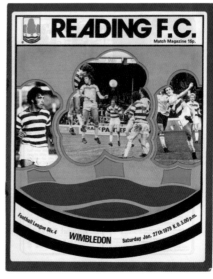

READING F.C.

Match Magazine 15p.

Football League Div. 4   **WIMBLEDON**   Saturday Jan. 27th 1979 K.O. 3.00 p.m.

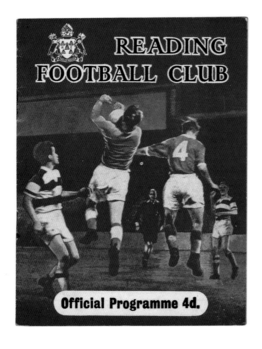

READING FOOTBALL CLUB

Official Programme 4d.

ROCHDALE

FOUNDED: 1907
GROUND: Spotland
NICKNAME: Dale

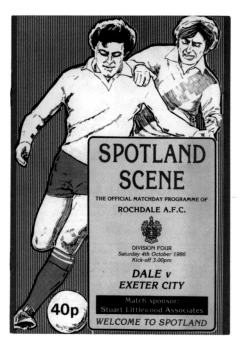

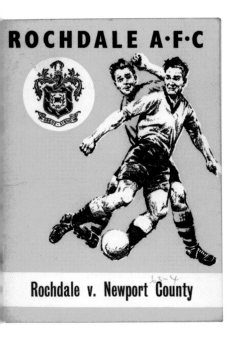

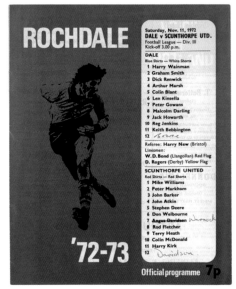

ROTHERHAM UNITED

FOUNDED: 1870
GROUND: Millmoor
NICKNAME: The Millers

SCARBOROUGH

FOUNDED: 1879
GROUND: Seamer Road
NICKNAME: The Seasiders, Seadogs, Boro

FA TROPHY WINNERS: 1973, 1976, 1977

SCUNTHORPE UNITED

FOUNDED: 1899
GROUND: Old Show Ground, Glanford Park
NICKNAME: The Iron
PREVIOUS NAME: Scunthorpe and Lindsay United

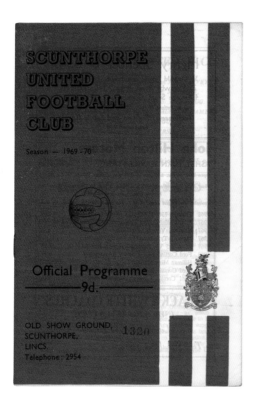

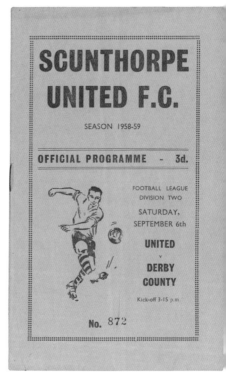

SHEFFIELD UNITED

FOUNDED: 1889
GROUND: Bramall Lane
NICKNAME: The Blades

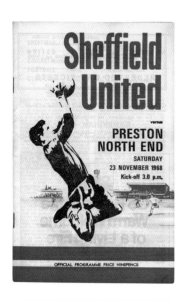

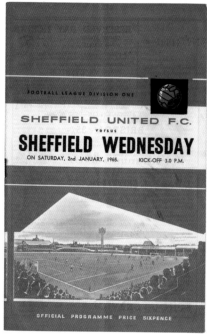

OFFICIAL PROGRAMME

4D

FOOTBALL LEAGUE
DIVISION I

SHEFFIELD UNITED
FOOTBALL CLUB

versus

EVERTON

KICK-OFF 7.30 p.m. WEDNESDAY, 14th MARCH, 1962.

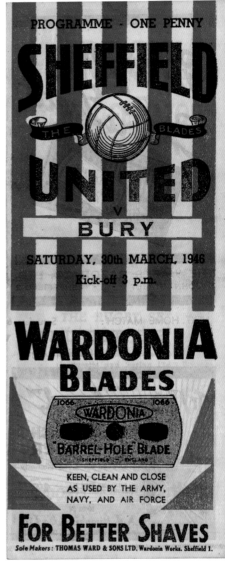

PROGRAMME - ONE PENNY

SHEFFIELD

THE BLADES

UNITED

v

BURY

SATURDAY, 30th MARCH, 1946

Kick-off 3 p.m.

WARDONIA
BLADES

1066   **WARDONIA**   1066
BARREL-HOLE BLADE
SHEFFIELD — ENGLAND

KEEN, CLEAN AND CLOSE
AS USED BY THE ARMY,
NAVY, AND AIR FORCE

FOR BETTER SHAVES

Sole Makers: THOMAS WARD & SONS LTD, Wardonia Works, Sheffield 1.

SHEFFIELD WEDNESDAY

FOUNDED: 1867
GROUND: Hillsborough
NICKNAME: The Owls

LEAGUE CUP WINNERS: 1991

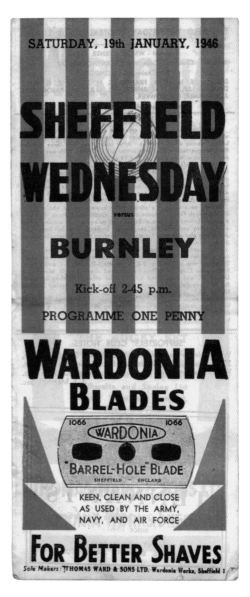

OFFICIAL PROGRAMME
PRICE SIXPENCE

SHEFFIELD WEDNESDAY
LEAGUE DIVISION ONE FOOTBALL
Hillsborough

SHEFFIELD WEDNESDAY
versus
MANCHESTER UNITED
ON SATURDAY, 24th AUGUST, 1963
KICK-OFF 3.0 P.M.

SHREWSBURY TOWN

FOUNDED: 1886
GROUND: Gay Meadow
NICKNAME: The Shrews

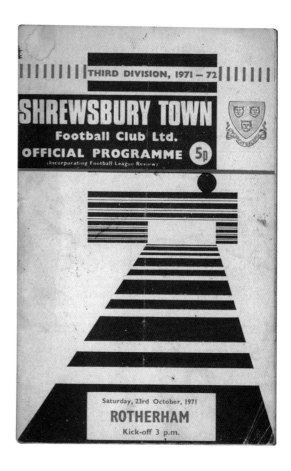

SOUTHAMPTON

FOUNDED: 1885
GROUND: The Dell
NICKNAME: The Saints

FA CUP WINNERS: 1976

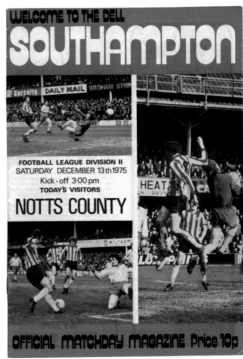

SOUTHEND UNITED

FOUNDED: 1906
GROUND: Roots Hall
NICKNAME: The Shrimpers

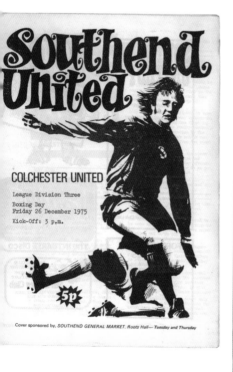

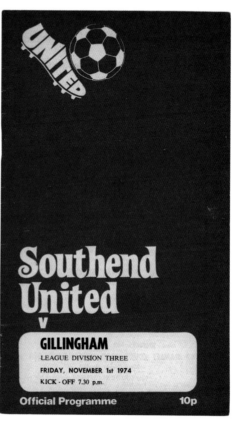

Official Programme 1/-

United v. Darlington

Football League Division 4. Kick-Off 7.30 p.m. Friday, 28th August, 1970.

SOUTHEND UNITED

WREXHAM

League Division 3
KICK OFF 7.30 p.m.
SATURDAY 12th AUGUST, 1972
PROGRAMME NO. 1

OFFICIAL PROGRAMME

Southend United

FOOTBALL LEAGUE
DIVISION THREE

v

WATFORD

Monday
1st January, 1979

Kick-off 3.00 p.m.

Today's Sponsor
Hoover

15p
Official Programme

SOUTHPORT

FOUNDED: 1881
GROUND: Haig Avenue
NICKNAME: The Sandgrounders

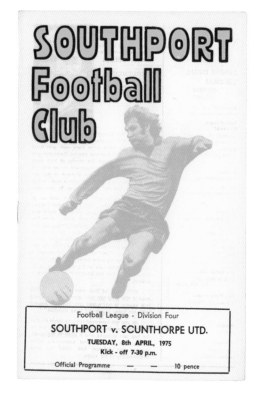

STOCKPORT COUNTY

FOUNDED: 1883
GROUND: Edgeley Park
NICKNAME: The Hatters

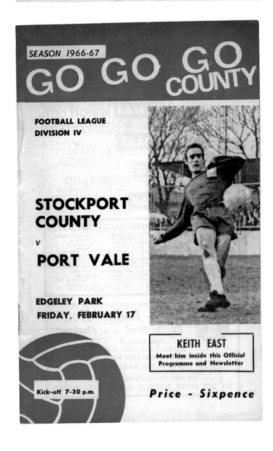

STOKE CITY

FOUNDED: 1863
GROUND: Victoria Ground
NICKNAME: The Potters

LEAGUE CUP WINNERS: 1972

SUNDERLAND

FOUNDED: 1879
GROUND: Roker Park
NICKNAME: The Rokerites

FA CUP WINNERS: 1973

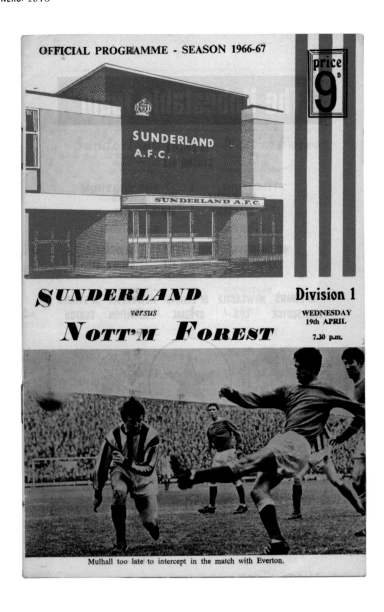

Mulhall too late to intercept in the match with Everton.

SWANSEA CITY

FOUNDED: 1912
GROUND: Vetch Field
NICKNAME: The Swans
PREVIOUS NAME: Swansea Town

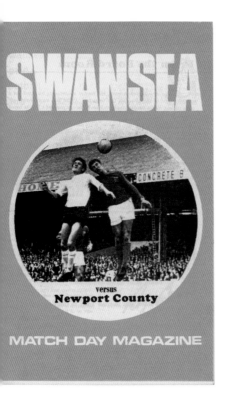

SWINDON TOWN

FOUNDED: 1881
GROUND: County Ground
NICKNAME: The Robins

LEAGUE CUP WINNERS: 1969

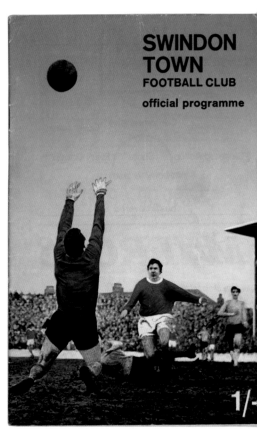

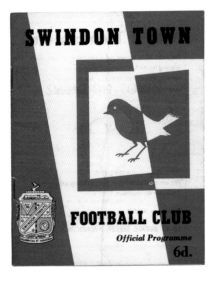

TORQUAY UNITED

FOUNDED: 1921
GROUND: Plainmoor
NICKNAME: The Gulls

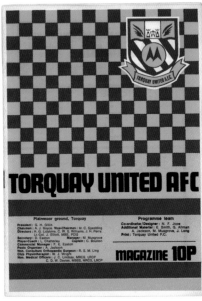

TOTTENHAM HOTSPUR

FOUNDED: 1882
GROUND: White Hart Lane
NICKNAME: Spurs

LEAGUE CHAMPIONS: 1951, 1961
FA CUP WINNERS: 1961, 1962, 1967, 1981, 1982
LEAGUE CUP WINNERS: 1971
UEFA CUP WINNERS: 1972
EUROPEAN CUP WINNERS' CUP WINNERS: 1963

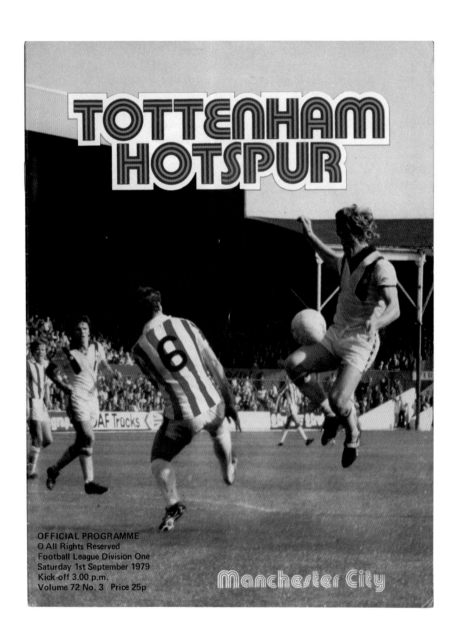

TOTTENHAM HOTSPUR

OFFICIAL PROGRAMME
© All Rights Reserved
Football League Division One
Saturday 1st September 1979
Kick-off 3.00 p.m.
Volume 72 No. 3   Price 25p

Manchester City

TRANMERE ROVERS

FOUNDED: 1884
GROUND: Prenton Park
NICKNAME: Rovers

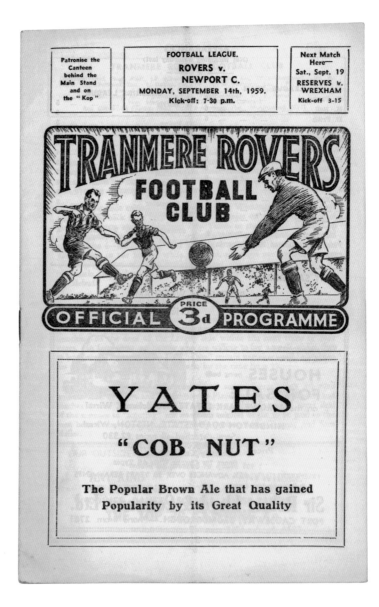

WALSALL

FOUNDED: 1888
GROUND: Fellows Park
NICKNAME: The Saddlers

WATFORD

FOUNDED: 1881
GROUND: Vicarage Road
NICKNAME: The Hornets

WATFORD
FOOTBALL
CLUB

SEASON 1969-70

(Graphic Photo)

Saturday, 7th February, 1970

F.A. CUP 5TH ROUND

GILLINGHAM

Kick-off 3.00 p.m.

OFFICIAL PROGRAMME   ONE SHILLING

WATFORD
FOOTBALL
CLUB

Official Programme 10p

STOCKPORT
COUNTY

Football League Division 4

Saturday, 4th October, 1975

Kick-off 3.00 p.m.

WEST BROMWICH ALBION

FOUNDED: 1879
GROUND: The Hawthorns
NICKNAME: The Trostles, Baggies

FA CUP WINNERS: 1954, 1968
LEAGUE CUP WINNERS: 1966

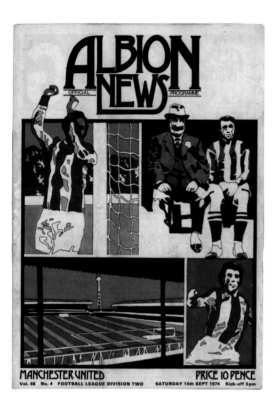

ALBION NEWS

OFFICIAL PROGRAMME

MANCHESTER UNITED   PRICE 10 PENCE

Vol. 66   No. 4   FOOTBALL LEAGUE DIVISION TWO   SATURDAY 14th SEPT 1974   Kick-off 3 pm

OFFICIAL ALBION ◉ NEWS

AND PROGRAMME

WEST BROMWICH ALBION FOOTBALL CLUB LIMITED

President Major H. Wilson Keys, M.C.T.D

Directors Mr J. W. Gaunt Chairman Mr T. W. Glidden Vice-Chairman
Mr L. Prichards Mr C. H. James Mr F. A. Millichip Mr T. H. Silk
Secretary Mr Alan Everiss, J.P Manager Mr G. A. Ashman

Ground The Hawthorns West Bromwich Grams 'Football West Bromwich' Phone 021-553 0095
Club Colours, Shirts—Navy Blue and White Stripes Shorts—White

Vol. 60. No. 46 (Copyright)   23rd April, 1969.

ALBION v IPSWICH TOWN

ONE SHILLING ●

ALBION NEWS

BOBBY HOPE TESTIMONIAL / ALBION v ATHLETICO BILBAO

WEST BROMWICH ALBION v ATHLETICO BILBAO/BOBBY HOPE TESTIMONIAL/WEDNESDAY APRIL 21/71/VOLUME 62 NUMBER 25/OFFICIAL MATCHDAY MAGAZINE PRICE 5p.
WEST BROMWICH ALBION FOOTBALL CLUB LIMITED, THE HAWTHORNS, WEST BROMWICH 021-553 0095. President MAJOR H. WILSON KEYS, M.C, T.D, Vice-President S. R. SHEPHARD, J.P.
Board of Directors Chairman J. W. GAUNT, Vice-Chairman F. A. MILLICHIP, T. W. GLIDDEN, L. PRICHARDS, T. H. SILK, J. GORDON, Secretary ALAN EVERISS, J.P. Manager ALAN ASHMAN
Promotions Manager LES THORLEY. Medical Officers J. H. KIRKHAM, F.R.C.S., Dr R. O. RIMMER, M.B., Ch.B., Dr F. BOTTOMLEY M.B.,Ch.B. Publicity G. BARTRAM

WEST HAM UNITED

FOUNDED: 1895
GROUND: Upton Park
NICKNAME: The Hammers

FA CUP WINNERS: 1964, 1975, 1980
EUROPEAN CUP WINNERS' CUP WINNERS: 1965

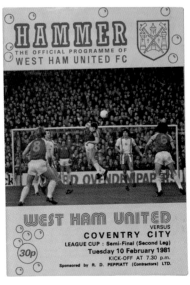

WIGAN ATHLETIC

FOUNDED: 1932
GROUND: Springfield Park
NICKNAME: The Latics

WIMBLEDON

FOUNDED: 1889
GROUND: Plough Lane
NICKNAME: The Dons

FA CUP WINNERS: 1988
FA AMATEUR CUP WINNERS: 1963

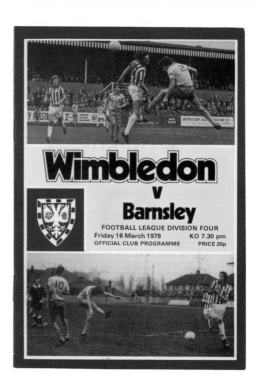

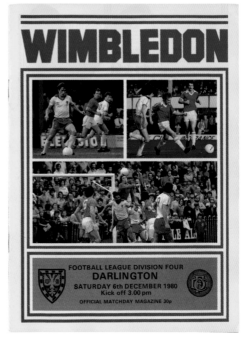

WOLVERHAMPTON WANDERERS

FOUNDED: 1877
GROUND: Molineux
NICKNAME: Wolves

LEAGUE CHAMPIONS: 1954, 1958, 1959
FA CUP WINNERS: 1949, 1960
LEAGUE CUP WINNERS: 1974, 1980

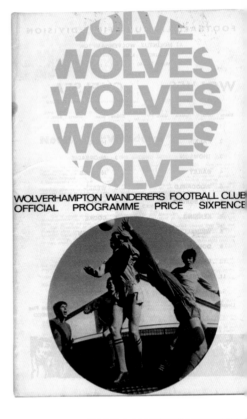

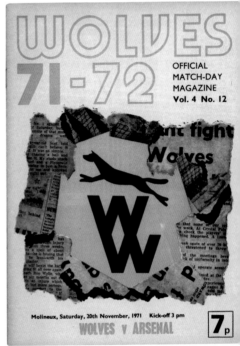

WORKINGTON

FOUNDED: 1884, reformed 1921
GROUND: Borough Park
NICKNAME: The Reds

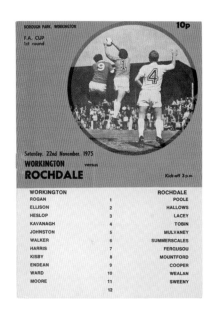

WORKINGTON		ROCHDALE
ROGAN	1	POOLE
ELLISON	2	HALLOWS
HESLOP	3	LACEY
KAVANAGH	4	TOBIN
JOHNSTON	5	MULVANEY
WALKER	6	SUMMERSCALES
HARRIS	7	FERGUSOU
KISBY	8	MOUNTFORD
ENDEAN	9	COOPER
WARD	10	WEALAN
MOORE	11	SWEENY
	12	

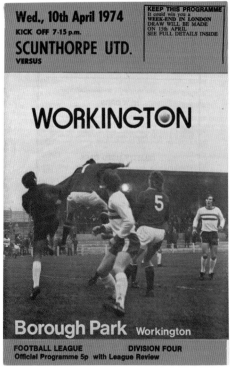

WREXHAM

FOUNDED: 1872
GROUND: Racecourse Ground
NICKNAME: The Robins, Red Dragons

YORK CITY

FOUNDED: 1922
GROUND: Bootham Crescent
NICKNAME: The Minstermen

YORK CITY FOOTBALL CLUB LTD

OFFICIAL
PROGRAMME
1/-

FOOTBALL LEAGUE - DIVISION IV

YORK C. v NEWPORT
SATURDAY, 28th DEC., 1968
KICK-OFF 3.00 p.m.

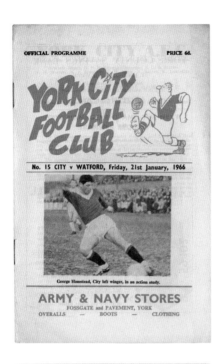

OFFICIAL PROGRAMME   PRICE 6d.

YORK CITY FOOTBALL CLUB

No. 15 CITY v WATFORD, Friday, 21st January, 1966

George Hanstead, City left winger, in an action study.

ARMY & NAVY STORES
FOSSGATE and PAVEMENT, YORK

OVERALLS — BOOTS — CLOTHING

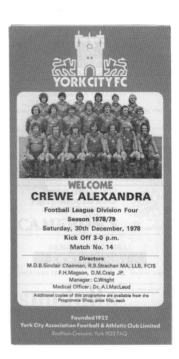

YORK CITY FC

WELCOME
CREWE ALEXANDRA

Football League Division Four
Season 1978/79
Saturday, 30th December, 1978
Kick Off 3-0 p.m.
Match No. 14

Directors
M.D.B.Sinclair *Chairman*, R.B.Strachan MA, LLB, FCIS
F.H.Magson, D.M.Craig JP.
Manager : C.Wright
Medical Officer: Dr. A.I.MacLeod

Additional copies of this programme are available from the
Programme Shop, price 10p. each

Founded 1922
York City Association Football & Athletic Club Limited
Bootham Crescent, York YO3 7AQ

YORK CITY

Match Number 6 Football League Division II
YORK CITY v OXFORD UNITED
Saturday 27th Sept. 1975 Kick off 3.00 p.m.

YORK CITY
(Maroon/White)

1 Graeme CRAWFORD
2 John STONE
3 Derrick DOWNING
4 John WOODWARD
5 Barry SWALLOW
6 Chris TOPPING
7 Brian POLLARD
8 Dennis WANN
9 Jimmy SEAL
10 Chris JONES
11 Eric McMORDIE
12

OXFORD UNITED
(Yellow/Blue)

1 Roy BURTON
2 Les TAYLOR
3 John SHUKER
4 Nick LOWE
5 Colin CLARKE
6 Max BRIGGS
7 Peter HOUSEMAN
8 Steve AYLOTT
9 Derek CLARKE
10 Mick TAIT
11 Brian HERON
12

OFFICIALS
Referee: J. RICE
(Leyland, Preston)
Linesmen:
Yellow Flag: A. F. JENKINS
(Scunthorpe)
Red Flag: D. SCOTT
(Burnley)

PRICE 10p

MATCH DAY PROGRAMME 1975-76 SEASON

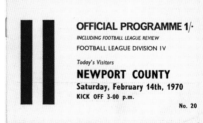

YORK CITY F.C.

OFFICIAL PROGRAMME 1/-
INCLUDING FOOTBALL LEAGUE REVIEW

FOOTBALL LEAGUE DIVISION IV

Today's Visitors

NEWPORT COUNTY

Saturday, February 14th, 1970
KICK OFF 3-00 p.m.

No. 20

NON-LEAGUE CLUBS   1945-1992

ALTRINCHAM

FOUNDED: 1903
GROUND: Moss Lane
NICKNAME: The Robins

FA TROPHY WINNERS: 1986

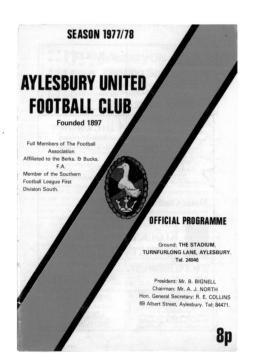

AYLESBURY UNITED

FOUNDED: 1897
GROUND: Buckingham Road
NICKNAME: The Ducks

BACUP BOROUGH

FOUNDED: 1875
GROUND: West View
NICKNAME: Boro

BEDFORD TOWN

FOUNDED: 1908, reformed 1989
GROUND: The Eyrie
NICKNAME: The Eagles

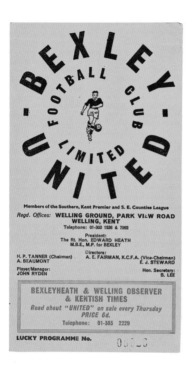

BEXLEY UNITED

FOUNDED: 1925, defunct 1976
GROUND: Park View Road
          (now used by Welling United)
NICKNAME: Town, The Kingfishers

BISHOP AUCKLAND

FOUNDED: 1886
GROUND: Kingsway
NICKNAME: Bishops

AMATEUR CUP WINNERS: 1955, 1956, 1957

BLYTH SPARTANS

FOUNDED: 1899
GROUND: Croft Park
NICKNAME: The Spartans

BOSTON UNITED

FOUNDED: 1933
GROUND: York Street
NICKNAME: The Pilgrims

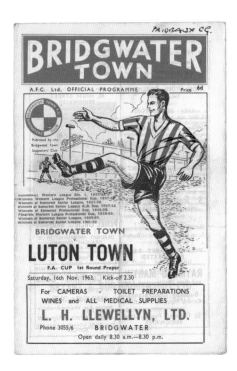

BRIDGWATER TOWN

FOUNDED: 1898, reformed 1946, 1984
GROUND: Castle Field, Fairfax Park
NICKNAME: The Robins

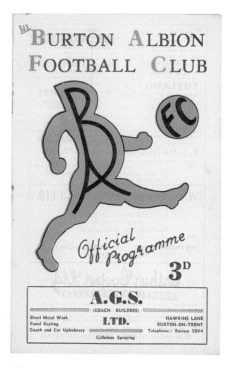

BURTON ALBION

FOUNDED: 1950
GROUND: Lloyds Foundry, Eton Park
NICKNAME: The Brewers

CAMBRIDGE CITY

FOUNDED: 1908
GROUND: Milton Road
NICKNAME: The Lilywhites

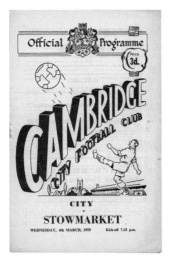

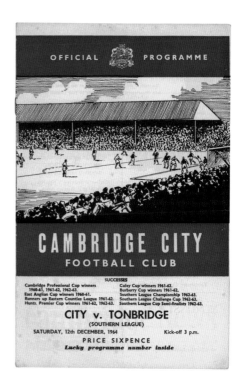

CARSHALTON ATHLETIC

FOUNDED: 1905
GROUND: War Memorial Sports Ground
NICKNAME: The Robins

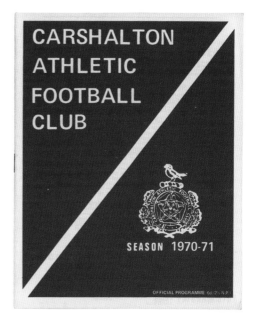

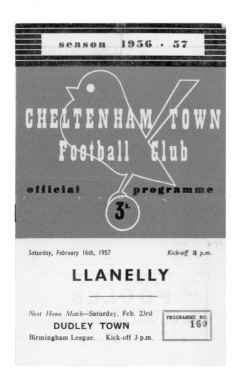

CHELTENHAM TOWN

FOUNDED: 1887
GROUND: Whaddon Road
NICKNAME: The Robins

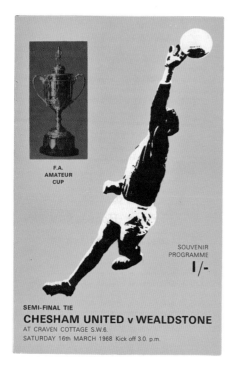

CHESHAM UNITED

FOUNDED: 1917
GROUND: The Meadow
NICKNAME: The Generals

CHORLEY

FOUNDED: 1883
GROUND: Victory Park
NICKNAME: The Magpies

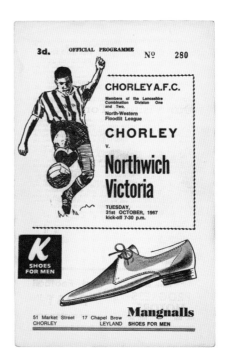

CORINTHIAN-CASUALS

FOUNDED: Corinthians 1882, Casuals 1883,
       amalgamated 1939
GROUND: King George's Field
NICKNAME: The Casuals

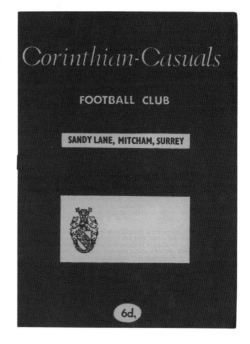

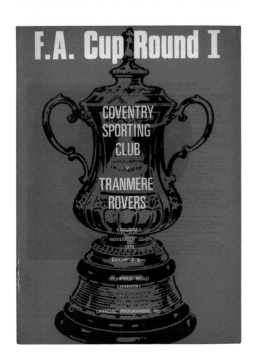

COVENTRY SPORTING CLUB

FOUNDED: 1946, defunct 1989
GROUND: Kirby Corner Road
NICKNAME: Sporting

DEAL TOWN

FOUNDED: 1908
GROUND: Charles Sports Ground
NICKNAME: Town

DOVER

FOUNDED: 1891, reformed as
Dover Athletic 1983
GROUND: Crabble
NICKNAME: The Whites

EAST GRINSTEAD TOWN

FOUNDED: 1890
GROUND: West Street, East Court
NICKNAME: The Wasps

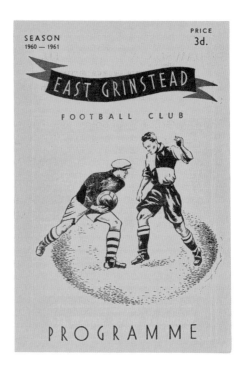

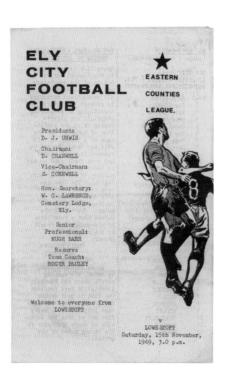

ELY CITY

FOUNDED: 1885
GROUND: Paradise Ground,
　　　　　Unwin Sports Ground
NICKNAME: The Robins

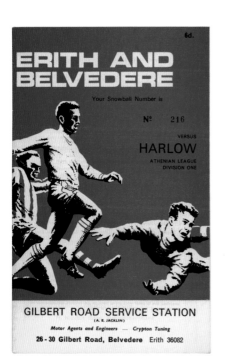

ERITH AND BELVEDERE

FOUNDED: 1922
GROUND: Park View
NICKNAME: The Deres

FINCHLEY

FOUNDED: 1874, amalgamated with Wingate
as Wingate & Finchley 1991
GROUND: Summers Lane
NICKNAME: The Blues

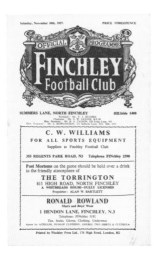

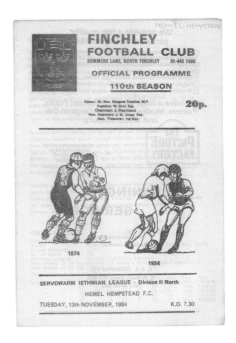

FOLKESTONE TOWN

FOUNDED: 1884, defunct 1991
GROUND: Cheriton Road
(now used by Folkestone Invicta)
NICKNAME: Town

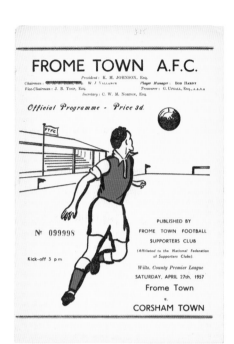

FROME TOWN

FOUNDED: 1904
GROUND: Badgers Hill
NICKNAME: The Robins

GOOLE TOWN

FOUNDED: 1900
GROUND: Victoria Pleasure Ground
NICKNAME: The Vikings

GUILDFORD CITY

FOUNDED: 1921
GROUND: Joseph's Road
NICKNAME: City

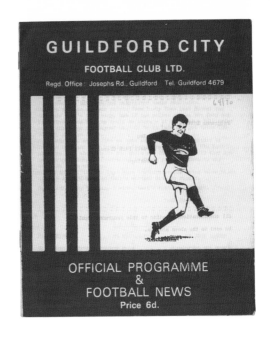

HAMPTON

FOUNDED: 1921
GROUND: The Beveree
NICKNAME: The Beavers

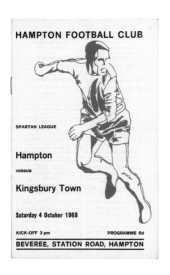

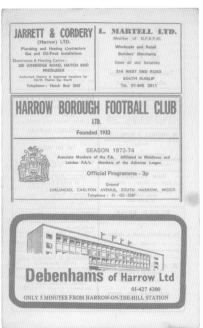

HARROW BOROUGH

FOUNDED: 1933
GROUND: Earlsmead
NICKNAME: The Boro

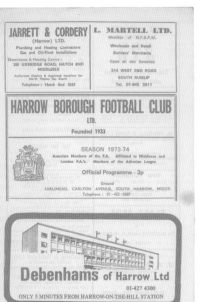

HARLOW TOWN

FOUNDED: 1879
GROUND: Old Harlow, Harlow Sports Centre
NICKNAME: The Hawks

HASTINGS UNITED

FOUNDED: 1894
GROUND: The Pilot Field
NICKNAME: The Arrows

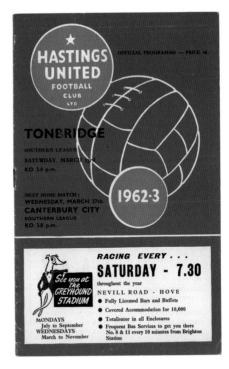

HATFIELD TOWN

FOUNDED: 1881
GROUND: Angerland Common
NICKNAME: Hats

HENDON

FOUNDED: 1908
GROUND: Claremont Road
NICKNAME: The Dons, Greens

FA AMATEUR CUP WINNERS: 1960, 1965, 1972

HERNE BAY

FOUNDED: 1886
GROUND: Winch's Field
NICKNAME: The Bay

HORSHAM

FOUNDED: 1871
GROUND: Queen Street
NICKNAME: The Hornets

HYDE UNITED

FOUNDED: 1919
GROUND: Ewen Fields
NICKNAME: The Tigers

ILFORD

FOUNDED: 1881, reformed 1987
GROUND: Lynn Road
NICKNAME: The Fords, Foxes

KETTERING TOWN

FOUNDED: 1872
GROUND: Rockingham Road
NICKNAME: The Poppies

LEATHERHEAD

FOUNDED: 1946
GROUND: Fetcham Grove
NICKNAME: The Tanners

LOCKHEED LEAMINGTON

FOUNDED: 1891
GROUND: Windmill Ground
NICKNAME: The Brakes

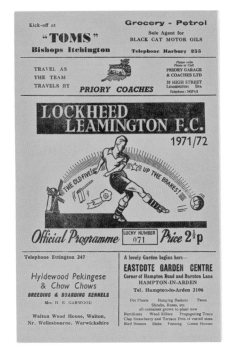

LOWESTOFT TOWN

FOUNDED: 1886
GROUND: Crown Meadow
NICKNAME: The Blues

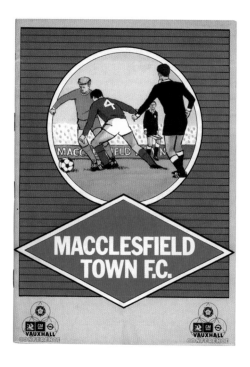

MACCLESFIELD TOWN

FOUNDED: 1874
GROUND: Moss Rose
NICKNAME: The Silkmen

FA TROPHY WINNERS: 1970

MALDON TOWN

FOUNDED: 1946
GROUND: Sadd's Ground
NICKNAME: The Blues

MALVERN TOWN

FOUNDED: 1947
GROUND: Langland Avenue
NICKNAME: Town

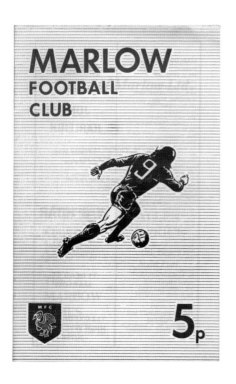

MARLOW

FOUNDED: 1870
GROUND: Alfred Davies Memorial Ground
NICKNAME: The Blues

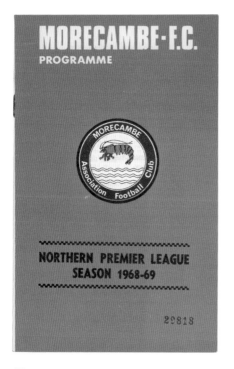

MORECAMBE

FOUNDED: 1920
GROUND: Christie Park
NICKNAME: The Shrimps

FA TROPHY WINNERS: 1974

NORTHWICH VICTORIA

FOUNDED: 1874
GROUND: Drill Field
NICKNAME: The Vics, Trickies

FA TROPHY WINNERS: 1984

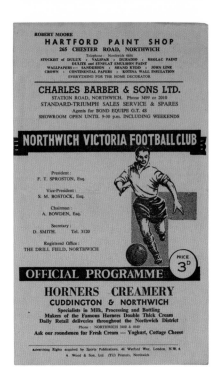

OXFORD CITY

FOUNDED: 1882
GROUND: White House Ground,
Cutteslowe Park
NICKNAME: City

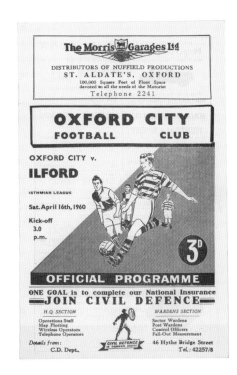

RAMSGATE ATHLETIC

FOUNDED: 1898
GROUND: Southwood Stadium
NICKNAME: The Rams

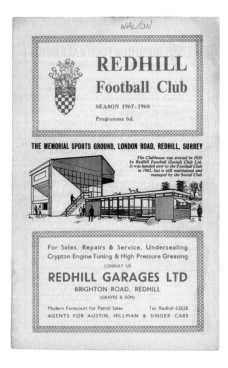

REDHILL

FOUNDED: 1894
GROUND: Memorial Ground, Kiln Brow
NICKNAME: The Lobsters

RHYL

FOUNDED: 1883
GROUND: Belle Vue
NICKNAME: The Lilywhites

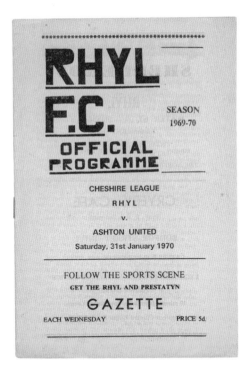

RUGBY TOWN

FOUNDED: 1956
GROUND: Butlin Road
NICKNAME: Valley

RUNCORN

FOUNDED: 1918
GROUND: Canal Street
NICKNAME: The Linnets

SHEPPEY UNITED

FOUNDED: 1890
GROUND: Botany Road
NICKNAME: The Ites

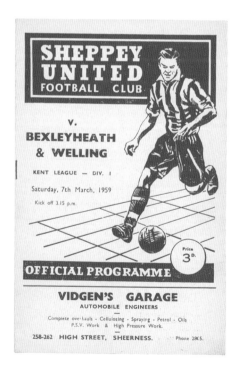

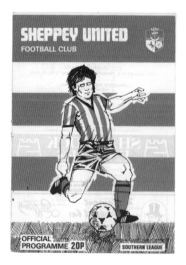

SHILDON

FOUNDED: 1890
GROUND: Dean Street
NICKNAME: The Railwaymen

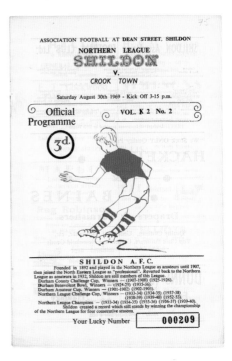

SKEGNESS TOWN

FOUNDED: 1947
GROUND: Burgh Road
NICKNAME: The Lilywhites

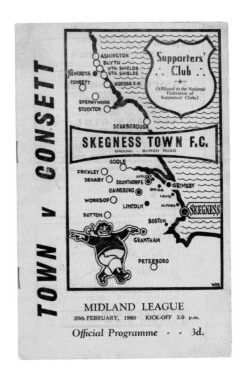

SKELMERSDALE UNITED

FOUNDED: 1882
GROUND: White Moss Park
NICKNAME: Skem

FA AMATEUR CUP WINNERS: 1971

SLOUGH TOWN

FOUNDED: 1890
GROUND: Wexham Park
NICKNAME: The Rebels

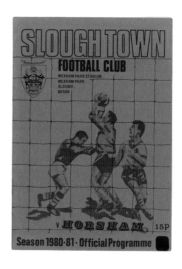

SOUTHALL

FOUNDED: 1871
GROUND: Western Road
NICKNAME: Hall

SOUTH BANK

FOUNDED: 1868
GROUND: Normanby Road
NICKNAME: The Bankers

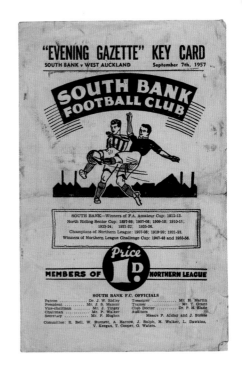

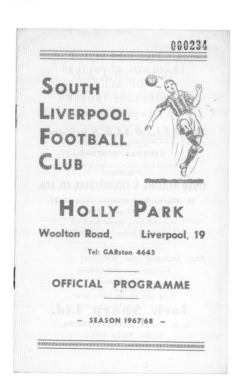

SOUTH LIVERPOOL

FOUNDED: 1910, reformed 1934
GROUND: Holly Park
NICKNAME: South

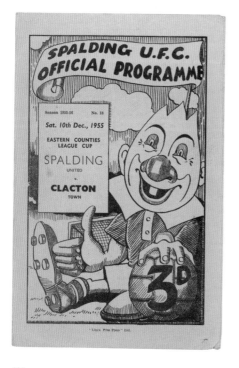

SPALDING UNITED

FOUNDED: 1921
GROUND: Sir Halley Stewart Field
NICKNAME: The Tulips

STAFFORD RANGERS

FOUNDED: 1876
GROUND: Marston Road
NICKNAME: The Boro

FA TROPHY WINNERS: 1972, 1979

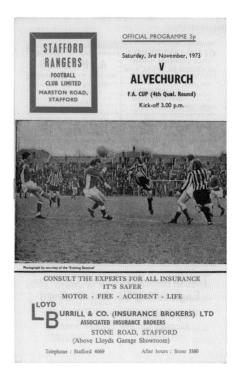

STAINES TOWN

FOUNDED: 1892
GROUND: Wheatsheaf Park
NICKNAME: The Swans

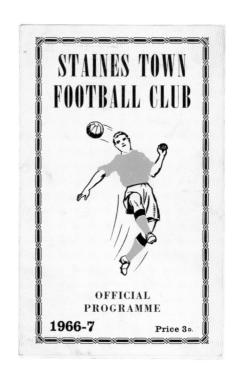

ST ALBANS CITY

FOUNDED: 1908
GROUND: Clarence Park
NICKNAME: The Saints

SUTTON UNITED

FOUNDED: 1898
GROUND: Gander Green Lane
NICKNAME: The U's

TAUNTON TOWN

FOUNDED: 1947
GROUND: Wordsworth Drive
NICKNAME: The Peacocks

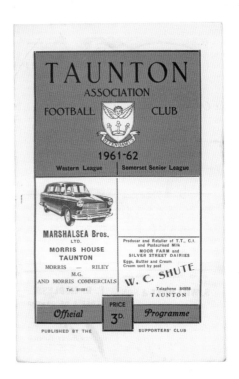

TELFORD UNITED

FOUNDED: 1872
GROUND: Bucks Head
NICKNAME: The Lilywhites

FA TROPHY WINNERS: 1971, 1983, 1989

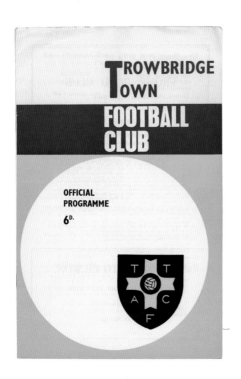

TROWBRIDGE TOWN

FOUNDED: 1880
GROUND: Woodmarsh
NICKNAME: Town

WALTHAMSTOW AVENUE

FOUNDED: 1900
GROUND: Green Pond Road
NICKNAME: Avenue

FA AMATEUR CUP WINNERS: 1952, 1961

WALTON & HERSHAM

FOUNDED: 1945
GROUND: Stompond Lane
NICKNAME: The Swans

FA AMATEUR CUP WINNERS: 1973

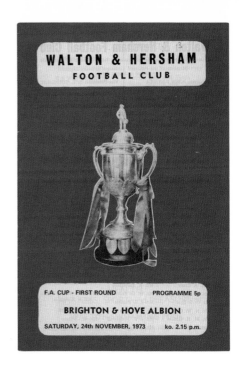

WEALDSTONE

FOUNDED: 1899
GROUND: Lower Mead
NICKNAME: The Stones, Royals

FA AMATEUR CUP WINNERS: 1966
FA TROPHY WINNERS: 1985

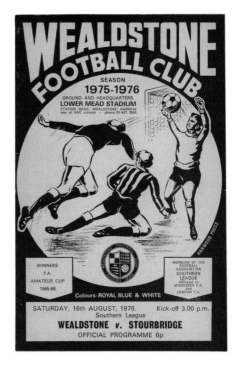

WELLINGBOROUGH TOWN

FOUNDED: 1867
GROUND: London Road
NICKNAME: The Doughboys

WORCESTER CITY

FOUNDED: 1902
GROUND: St George's Lane
NICKNAME: City

WYCOMBE WANDERERS

FOUNDED: 1884
GROUND: Loakes Park, Adams Park
NICKNAME: The Chairboys, Blues

FA TROPHY WINNERS: 1991

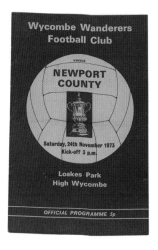

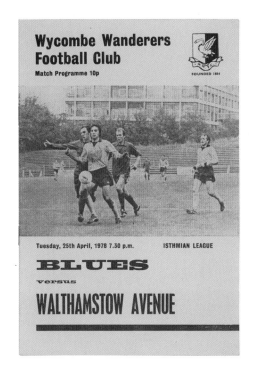

YEOVIL TOWN

FOUNDED: 1895
GROUND: The Huish, Huish Park
NICKNAME: The Glovers

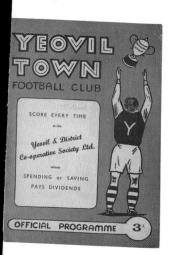

Bob Stanley was born in Horsham, Sussex, in 1964. A career in town planning was sidelined when he began freelance music writing with *NME* and *Melody Maker* in the late eighties, before forming the group Saint Etienne with childhood friend Pete Wiggs in 1990. This led to him achieving one of his two lifelong dreams – to appear in the FA Cup final or on *Top Of The Pops*. He has written for *The Times*, *The Guardian* and *Mojo*, and curated several film seasons at the Barbican. He still owns a 1975 Leatherhead rosette.

Paul Kelly left school at fifteen and trained to become a pilot, but a love of music kept him earthbound. After playing guitar with his band East Village in the eighties he took up sleeve design and photography, working with groups including Primal Scream and The Magic Numbers. His longstanding association with Saint Etienne has led onto several film projects including *Finisterre* and the football films *Bound For Glory* and *Monty The Lamb*. He claims to support Wycombe Wanderers.

Thanks to:
David Allcock, Owen Clarke, Tom Crussell, Richard Dawson, Bernard Gallagher, Brian Glanville, Ian Hands, Adrian Lobb, Alex Noble, David Shukman, D.J. Taylor, Richard Whitehead